BEAD ON A WIRE

MAKING HANDCRAFTED WIRE AND BEADED JEWELRY

Sharilyn Miller

NORTH LIGHT BOOKS

CINCINNATI, OHIO
www.artistsnetwork.com

Dedication

I would like to dedicate this special book to my students, who motivate and inspire me every day. The ancient techniques found in *Bead on a Wire* have been passed down for centuries from one artist to the next. I hope that by offering this book to a contemporary audience, many new hands will take up the craft of wire-art jewelry. By applying their own intelligence and creativity to the task, these artists will eventually come up with innovative designs and techniques, thus expanding an art form that will bring joy to future generations of jewelry artists. Maybe someday I'll take a workshop from one of you. I hope so!

11 10 09 08 07   8 7 6 5 4

Library of Congress Cataloging-in-Publication Data

Miller, Sharilyn.
  Bead on a wire / Sharilyn Miller.-- 1st ed.
    p. cm.
  Includes index.
  ISBN-13: 978-1-58180-650-2 (pbk. : alk. paper)
  ISBN-10: 1-58180-650-7 (pbk. : alk. paper)
  1. Beadwork. 2. Jewelry making. 3. Wire craft. I. Title.

TT860.M56 2005
745.594'2--dc22

fw

F+W PUBLICATIONS, INC.

Editor: Jennifer Fellinger

Designer: Stephanie Goodrich

Layout Artists: Kathy Gardner, Leigh Ann Lentz

Production Coordinator: Robin Richie

Photographers: Christine Polomsky, Sylvia Bissonnette

Styled photography: Sylvia Bissonnette
      (949) 261-2207
      www.sylviabissonnette.com

Metric Conversion Chart

To convert	to	multiply by
Inches	Centimeters	2.54
Centimeters	Inches	0.4
Feet	Centimeters	30.5
Centimeters	Feet	0.03
Yards	Meters	0.9
Meters	Yards	1.1
Sq. Inches	Sq. Centimeters	6.45
Sq. Centimeters	Sq. Inches	0.16
Sq. Feet	Sq. Meters	0.09
Sq. Meters	Sq. Feet	10.8
Sq. Yards	Sq. Meters	0.8
Sq. Meters	Sq. Yards	1.2
Pounds	Kilograms	0.45
Kilograms	Pounds	2.2
Ounces	Grams	28.3
Grams	Ounces	0.035

ABOUT THE Author

Sharilyn Miller is an art instructor who conducts jewelry workshops across the United States, Canada, Mexico and Europe. She is the author of *Stamp Art* (1999) and *The Stamp Artist's Project Book* (2001). Her third book, *Rubber Stamped Jewelry* (2003), was published by North Light Books. Sharilyn's jewelry is sold in galleries and resides in collections across North America and Europe.

Sharilyn also is Editor-in-Chief and founding editor of two magazines, *Belle Armoire* (art to wear) and *Art Doll Quarterly*. She created and launched *Belle Armoire* in 2001 and *Art Doll Quarterly* in 2003. She was Editor-in-Chief of Somerset Studio magazine (paper arts, art stamping, and calligraphy) from 1996 to 2004. Prior to working in the craft magazine industry, Sharilyn was a reporter with *The Orange County Register* in Santa Ana, California. She holds a commercial art degree from Northwest College of Art, Poulsbo, Washington, and a bachelor's degree in print journalism communications from California State University, Fullerton.

Visit Sharilyn's website at **www.SharilynMiller.com**.

Acknowledgments

A book of this nature owes its existence to a team of creative individuals, for many people besides the author have had their hands in its creation. I would like to personally thank editorial director Tricia Waddell, who believed in this project from the start and encouraged me to write a book on wire-art jewelry. Craft editor Jennifer Fellinger made the process of producing this book a real joy, and photographer Christine Polomsky kept us all in good humor during the step-out photo shoot while producing excellent close-up shots—not an easy task. Special thanks are also due to photographer Sylvia Bissonnette, whose gorgeous photography makes my jewelry look good!

I would be remiss if I did not also thank some very special people who have taught me a lot about making and designing jewelry with wire. First, my friend Louise Duhamel, a jewelry artist from Carlsbad, California, who taught me much about design principles and how to choose beads for jewelry. She also taught me how to make the Delicate Pendant found on pages 88–89. My friend Joyce Boyd-Wells of San Diego, California, came up with the idea of using two *S* clasps in a necklace design to make Convertible Jewelry. Connie Fox, another San Diego-based jewelry artist and teacher, inspires me greatly with her chunky, ethnic bangle bracelets. But above all, I must thank wire guru Lynne Merchant of Encinitas, California, who has taught generations of grateful jewelry designers by sharing her knowledge of the craft.

TABLE OF Contents

Introduction • 6   The Jewelry Toolkit • 8

TECHNIQUES • 14

PROJECTS • 60

INTRODUCTION

So, you want to learn how to make fine jewelry with wire and beads? You've come to the right place.

Outside of workshops (by far the best way to learn), instructional DVDs and videos, I think you'll find this book to be one of the best avenues to success in making beautiful body ornaments to wear and enjoy.

There are several reasons why I love making wire-based jewelry. First, I feel empowered when I pick up a piece of plain round wire and a few simple hand tools to fashion a thing of beauty. To gaze upon something you've made with your own two hands is quite gratifying—a real boost to your self-esteem.

I also appreciate the fact that I can make jewelry to complement anything in my wardrobe. Because I make it myself, my jewelry fits my body and my lifestyle. It also fits my mood. Sometimes I feel like wearing bold and earthy jewelry, with an ethnic style and the appearance of great age. At other times I prefer wearing a more contemporary piece, or something light and delicate that goes with spring and summer outfits. Fashioning necklaces to fit the necklines of favorite garments, creating matching earrings and bracelets at a fraction of the cost of purchasing fine jewelry sets, and making high-quality gifts for friends and relatives are just some of the many benefits of making jewelry yourself.

Another benefit to making jewelry with wire is that you don't need a lot of expensive tools or dangerous equipment. For instance, I never solder my jewelry—not even my jump rings! Once you know how to make components (such as jump rings, clasps, links and bead wraps) correctly, there is no need to solder them. The only electric tools I use are a drill (to twist wire) and a bead reamer, which is useful when bead holes are too small to allow the wire to pass through them.

You won't need any caustic chemicals, either. In fact, the only chemical I ever use on my jewelry is liver of sulfur. Admittedly, it's a bit smelly, but it's perfectly safe to handle and dispose of. I never use a torch, never touch a rolling mill. There's nothing wrong with these tools or processes; I just prefer to keep things simple. Wire allows me to do that.

Immediate gratification is another reason why I so enjoy making jewelry with wire. Unlike the metalsmith, who may spend hours or even days creating a single item, the wire artist can make hundreds of pieces and components in the same amount of time. For instance, I can fashion a beautiful pair of earrings in less than five minutes—and so can you, once you've read this book and tried the techniques offered.

The sheer versatility of wire for jewelry making is quite astonishing. The possibilities of this medium are virtually unlimited, and the jewelry artist can spend a lifetime making interesting wire-based ornaments without exhausting all of its potential. As an artist, I have restricted myself to round wire because I want to thoroughly explore this medium before moving on to other types of wire, such as square, triangular and half-round.

I also have avoided using 14-karat or gold-filled wire because it's much more expensive than sterling silver, copper or brass—but there is no reason why you can't experiment with other types of wire yourself. In fact, I encourage you to explore all the possibilities that the world of wire has to offer. Are you ready? Let's get started!

You will need a basic jewelry toolkit containing the essential tools and materials used when making fine-art jewelry with wire. Although not all tools will be necessary for every project in this book, you should make a habit of keeping all your tools together in one place, ready at a moment's notice to use whenever the creative mood strikes.

Makeup bag with clear compartments

Search your local drug store for a makeup bag with clear compartments that zip up. It's handy for storing small tools, and the clear plastic makes it easy to find what you need without having to empty the entire bag.

Chasing hammer

A chasing hammer is essential for forging wire links. It has a large, smooth face for planishing (flattening) wire and sheet metal, and a smaller, rounder, ball-peen end used for riveting and creating small dimples in wire and sheet metal. Chasing hammers are also useful for striking chasing tools to make marks in sheet metal. Look for one with a slightly convex surface on a large smooth face, as a perfectly flat hammer will not create a smooth transition between the forged wire and the round wire; it will instead create an unsightly ridge.

Hard-plastic mallet
(rawhide mallet may be substituted)

A hard-plastic or rawhide mallet is very useful for work-hardening wire and sheet metal and for hammering out kinks without planishing or flattening the wire. It is also helpful when making wire links that become crooked due to manipulation. Look for a hammer that is well balanced and lightweight in your hand.

Jeweler's bench block, *measuring 2½" x 2½" (6cm x 6cm) or 4" x 4" (10cm x 10cm)*

Look for a block made of solid "tool" steel, ground smooth and flat, polished, and case-hardened. Jeweler's bench blocks are used for hammering wire and sheet metal with both hard-plastic mallets and chasing hammers. Be sure to purchase one that is solid steel, not one made partially of wood.

Pillow for bench block

To muffle the sound of hammering and to keep the bench block in place, use a "pillow." It looks like a bean bag, but is filled instead with either jewelry shot or with BBs. To make one, cut out two 6" (15cm) diameter circles from a piece of suede leather or heavy denim. Stitch the

Your Jewelry Toolkit

Below is a list of the tools and materials I find indispensable for making wire-based jewelry. For further clarification, pages 8–12 feature a description of each object. Depending on your needs, you may wish to add your own favorite tools to the toolkit.

Makeup bag with clear compartments	Hard-wire diagonal cutters
Chasing hammer	Hardware-store nails in sizes 1-gauge and 2-gauge
Hard-plastic mallet	Knitting needles in various sizes
Jeweler's bench block, measuring 2½" × 2½" (6cm × 6cm) or 4" × 4" (10cm × 10cm)	Wooden dowels
Pillow for bench block	Measuring tape
Ring mandrel	6" (15cm) flexible ruler
Ring-mandrel holder	Black indelible marking pen
Jeweler's saw frame with blades	Portable notebook and pen
Wire-gauge measuring tool	Electric bead reamer
Flat-nose pliers	Small pieces of rubber shelf liner
Chain-nose pliers	Electric drill with keyless chuck
Small round-nose pliers	Liver of sulfur
Extra-long round-nose pliers	Ultra-fine steel wool (0000 grade)
Bent-nose pliers	Rock tumbler with stainless-steel mixed jewelry shot and burnishing compound
Jewelry "needle" files: flat, round, triangular	Polishing cloth
Flush cutters	

9

circles together with a ¼″ (6mm) seam, leaving a 2″ (5cm) opening. Fill the bag two-thirds full of BBs or jewelry shot, and then stitch the opening closed. The pillow is now ready for use; place it beneath the bench block whenever you hammer wire or sheet metal.

Ring mandrel

Rings in half-sizes from 1 to 16 are formed on ring mandrels, which are used to size and shape wire or metal. These mandrels come in different shapes: round and smooth-tapered, round and stepped, grooved, flat-sided, square and finger-shaped. For most purposes, a round and smooth-tapered metal ring mandrel will suit your needs. I use them to make rings and hoop earrings, too.

An optional tool is a necklace mandrel. Shaped like a woman's neck and upper-chest area, necklace mandrels are used to shape, size and hammer wire or metal to create rigid torque-style neck wires for chokers and slider necklaces. A necklace mandrel makes it easy to shape necklaces and adjust them for size.

Ring-mandrel holder

If you're working alone, a ring-mandrel holder is handy. It frees your hands and provides support by holding both ends of the ring mandrel in place while you wrap wire around it. A mandrel holder can be bolted securely to a worktable for added stability.

Jeweler's saw frame with blades

Use a jeweler's saw to cut through sheet metal and heavy-gauge wire. Many different frames from different manufacturers around the world are available; buy the best frame you can afford. Steel saw blades are sold separately and are interchangeable; they are also very inexpensive.

Wire-gauge measuring tool

A British standard wire gauge is used to measure sheet metal and wire in gauges from 0 (very large) to 36 (extremely fine). The slots in the tool, not the holes, measure the gauge.

Flat-nose pliers

Used to grip wire for spiraling and other tasks, these pliers have a flat edge at the jaw tips. Use them to bend wire into sharp angles, to hold small links, to open and close jump rings (sideways), and for close work.

Chain-nose pliers

These pliers are similar to flat-nose pliers except that they come to a sharp point at the jaw tips and have a smooth, rounded outer surface on the jaws. Use them to grip wire, for spiraling wire and for other tasks requiring close work.

Clockwise from lower left: extra-long round-nose pliers, chain-nose pliers, small round-nose pliers, flat-nose pliers, bent-nose pliers, jeweler's saw, flat file, triangular file, round file, flush cutters, hard-wire diagonal cutters, wire-gauge measuring tool

Small round-nose pliers

These pliers are rounded with cone-shaped jaws that taper to points at the tips. Their short jaws give them maximum leverage for short work such as starting wire spirals. For working at the tip of the jaw, shorter round-nose pliers are best. These pliers are also useful for making small jump rings and rounded bends in wire for small links and ear wires.

Extra-long round-nose pliers

These pliers are similar to small round-nose pliers, except that they are quite a bit longer in the jaw, making them ideal for bending rounded wire to make ear wires and large jump rings. They are not as useful for starting wire spirals because they don't have the same leverage in the tips of the jaws as small round-nose pliers; also, they don't taper to as fine a point. Extra-long round-nose pliers are very useful, however, for many bench tasks and are the ideal all-purpose tool.

Bent-nose pliers

These pliers are similar to chain-nose pliers, but the jaw tips are bent at right angles to the tool.

tip

When buying any kind of jewelry pliers, always look for pliers made with top-grade steel, smooth jaws, a box joint and handles that fit comfortably in your hand.

Jewelry "needle" files: flat, round, triangular

Files are used to remove tool marks from wire and to polish the surface to remove burrs and other unsightly marks. It's most economical to purchase the best quality files you can afford, rather than to buy cheap files that won't last as long. The files are designed to be used in one direction.

Flush cutters

Suited for cutting 16- to 14-gauge wire, flush cutters, sometimes called "micro cutters," create a nice flush cut necessary for making many jewelry components.

Hard-wire diagonal cutters

These cutters are generally suited for cutting 14- to 12-gauge wire. They also provide a flush cut on one end of the wire and a beveled cut on the opposite end.

Nails, knitting needles and wooden dowels

These tools are useful for making wire coils in various sizes, which can then be cut into jump rings. Hardware-store nails in sizes 1-and 2-gauge can be used for extra-large jump rings, and knitting needles can be used to coil heavier gauge wire. The wire can sometimes dig into the soft wooden surface of dowels, making it difficult to remove the coiled wire. For this reason, take care not to wind wire too tightly around dowels.

Measuring tape

A measuring tape is useful for measuring large quantities of wire for coiling.

6" (15cm) flexible ruler

A shorter ruler is best for measuring links and bead wraps for small projects.

Black indelible marking pen

Use this pen to mark the wire where it's been measured prior to cutting it. Pens are also useful for marking your pliers when you need to place the wire in the same spot on the tool to make identical jump rings and other wire links. If you take jewelry-making lessons or use your tools in a public place, use the pen to write your name on everything you own.

Portable notebook and pen

You should keep a small notebook and pen with you at all times while designing new jewelry pieces. It's important to keep notes while you work because, in the heat of the moment, you may forget essential information, such as how many inches of wire were required to make a new link you've designed. This information will be of great use weeks or months later when you need to duplicate a jewelry piece and have forgotten how it was made. If you intend to sell your jewelry, record sources for beads, wire and tools, plus information on the length of time it took to create a particular jewelry piece and the cost of your materials.

Electric bead reamer

Bead reamers are used to enlarge holes in stone beads and pearls. Electric bead reamers are designed to be used with the tip submerged in water to keep the bead or pearl from over-heating and shattering. Note that they are not designed to create new holes in undrilled objects. Never try reaming a glass bead because it will shatter. If the bead reamer should slip from your hand while reaming a bead or pearl, unplug it first before removing it from the water.

Small pieces of rubber shelf liner

These are helpful when coiling wire. Start the coil as described in the *Techniques* section (pages 26–27). After a few wraps, grip the coil with a piece of rubber shelf liner. This should keep the coil from spinning as you continue wrapping it.

Electric drill with keyless chuck

You'll need an electric drill to twist wire, as described in the *Techniques* section (pages 22–23). (A battery-operated drill is fine.) Be sure to get one with lots of torque to make a tight twist. A keyless chuck is much easier to handle than a chuck that requires a key.

11

Clockwise from lower left: knitting needles, notebook and marking pen, electric bead reamer, cordless drill with keyless chuck, measuring tape, flexible ruler, hardware store nails, cut pieces of shelf liner, wooden dowels, ring mandrel, knitting needles

Liver of sulfur

This material is one of the most effective solutions for artificially aging sterling silver, fine silver, copper and brass by oxidation. To work, either the liver of sulfur or the jewelry piece itself must be hot; for this reason, it's important to mix dry chunks of liver of sulfur in hot (but not boiling) water and/or submerge the metal jewelry piece in very hot water before dipping it in the solution. Once submerged, metal jewelry will turn different colors, eventually becoming a deep gunmetal-gray or nearly black. Copper wire and metal turn pure black very quickly, while brass turns dark brown. Liver of sulfur is available in dry and wet solutions; the most economical form is dry hard pieces, which should not be exposed to moisture or sunlight prior to use. To see how liver of sulfur is used to darken metal jewelry, refer to the *Techniques* section (pages 57–58).

Ultra-fine steel wool (0000 grade)

Found in hardware stores and auto-body repair shops, 0000 steel wool is ultrafine and suitable for polishing metal jewelry. It can be used to polish and clean bare wire as well as finished jewelry pieces because it's very effective at removing surface grime and stickiness. For this reason, cleaning and straightening your wire prior to use is a good habit to get into. Ultra-fine steel wool is also useful for polishing away the blackening effect of liver of sulfur. While the material takes off the surface blackening, the grooves and details of the finished jewelry piece remain black. For a demonstration on using 0000 steel wool to polish metal jewelry, see the *Techniques* section (page 58).

Rock tumbler with stainless-steel mixed jewelry shot and burnishing compound

Once you've artificially aged your jewelry pieces in a liver-of-sulfur solution and polished away most of the surface blackening with steel wool, you're ready to polish and brighten them in a tumbler. A simple rock tumbler with a rubber barrel and a metal screw-tight lid is best. To use the tumbler, fill it about halfway with stainless-steel mixed jewelry shot, then about two-thirds full with tap water. Add a capful of liquid burnishing compound. Add the jewelry pieces until the barrel is full, then screw the lid on tight and tumble the barrel for 20 minutes. The jewelry will emerge bright and shiny.

Polishing cloth

Use a Sunshine cloth to polish silver, gold, brass, copper or bronze jewelry.

Clockwise from lower left: 0000 steel wool, liver of sulfur, rock tumbler, rubber barrel with mixed stainless steel jewelry shot, Sunshine polishing cloth

A Few More Supplies

An assortment of beads, charms, pendants and wire

Wire

Wire is available in various shapes (such as round and square) and patterns (such as flat and pre-twisted). It is also available in a variety of materials. In this book, all the projects are made with round wire in various gauges. I recommend practicing with copper or brass wire, both of which are sold inexpensively in hardware and jewelry supply stores. Easy to shape and manipulate, copper wire can be hammered until quite thin. Brass wire, which imitates the look of fine gold at a fraction of the cost, is a little stiffer than copper; but with the right tools, it too can be manipulated very easily.

Sterling silver–my favorite–may be a bit pricier than copper or brass, but its gorgeous look makes my jewelry easier to sell at higher prices. Sterling is soft enough to manipulate, but holds its shape well once it has been formed. While nickel silver is acceptable for practice, I prefer sterling or fine silver for making finished pieces. Durable and attractive, gold-filled wire is made by fusing a layer of 12-karat gold to a suitable supporting metal. The bond between the two metals is permanent, making gold-filled wire identical in appearance to solid 14-karat gold, yet much more economical.

Wire is measured by diameter, which is indicated by gauge numbers. The lower the gauge, the thicker the wire. For example, 12- or 14-gauge wire is rather heavy, ideal for making bangles and chokers; 10-gauge wire is almost too thick and stiff to handle; and 26-gauge is very fine, almost like hair, well-suited for coiling embellishments. Two of my favorite gauges are 16- and 18-gauge. I use the heavier 16-gauge wire for making jump rings and links for necklaces and bracelets, and the 18-gauge wire for adding embellishments and finer links.

Beads, Charms and Pendants

If you love making jewelry, chances are you already have a passion for beads, charms and pendants. There are no restrictions on the type, size, shape or color of these items for jewelry-making. However, when selecting beads for wire jewelry, you should pay close attention to the bead-hole size because most wire you'll be using is thicker than thread. This is particularly true for beaded bangles, which are designed on a mandrel wire of either 14- or 12-gauge diameter. When shopping for beads, I often bring a few small pieces of wire in various gauges, then use them to test the sizes of the holes on those beads I'm most interested in.

Also look for lightweight beads and charms because their weight adds significantly to the heft of your finished jewelry pieces. I'm particularly careful about the size and weight of beads and charms I select for making earrings, because no one likes having their earlobes dragged down by heavy beads.

Techniques

Good technique is the foundation of superior jewelry design and manufacture. There really is no substitute! Fortunately, you will find some excellent instruction on this topic right here in the *Techniques* section.

Start with the simple steps shown on the first few pages–holding your pliers correctly, and cleaning, cutting, measuring and marking your wire–mimicking the step-by-step photos provided. Refer to these instructions and photographs frequently as you progress through the lessons on the following pages. Here you'll find instruction on all the fundamental skills you need to make beautiful, durable jewelry pieces: hammering wire, making spirals and jump rings, twisting wire, making eye pins, coiling wire for bead wraps, and fashioning wrapped eye pins, bead dangles, bead connectors, caged beads, wire links, clasps and pendant suspenders.

TECHNIQUE 1 Working With Jewelry Pliers

If you're new to wire jewelry, you might find it a bit challenging at first to handle your pliers skillfully. By holding them in your hand correctly and using the method illustrated below to open and close your pliers, you can turn these unfamiliar tools into a natural extension of your hands. Practice handling them as described, and soon this skill will become second nature to you.

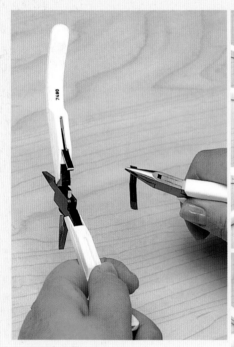

Preparing jewelry pliers. When I buy a new pair of pliers, I always remove the springs to give the pliers more freedom of movement. Open the pliers until fully extended, as shown. Then, use another pair of pliers to pull out the springs from the inside of the handles. Spray with a lubricant such as WD-40 and work it into the crevices.

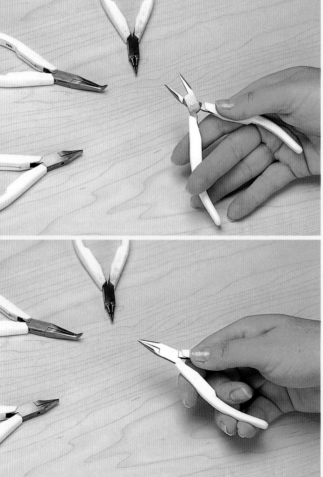

Holding pliers open. Use your middle finger to open your jewelry pliers.

Holding pliers closed. Steady your pliers with your middle finger and use your other three fingers to close them.

Cleaning and Cutting Wire

Cleaning and cutting wire are two fundamental skills you will use every time you make a piece of wire jewelry. Make it your habit to carefully clean your wire before working with it. Your wire might look clean and shiny, but chances are that it has attracted dirt and grime from repeated handling. Some wire manufacturers place white tape around the spools of wire prior to shipping, and the sticky residue from this tape must be removed from the wire before you can make jewelry.

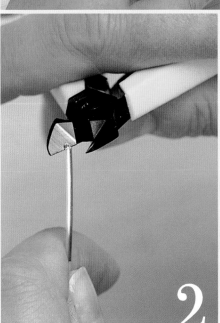

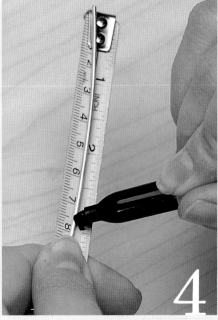

1 CLEAN WIRE

Before measuring and cutting a length of wire, always clean the wire. Tear off a chunk of 0000 steel wool, and then roll the steel wool between the palms of your hands to compress the fibers. Rub the compressed steel wool along the length of the wire. The steel wool will clean, polish and straighten the wire without scratching it.

2 PREPARE TO CUT WIRE

Start by flush cutting the wire to remove any wedge-shaped ends that may skew the measurement. To do so, place the end of the wire in the middle of the flush cutters, where you have the most leverage.

3 FLUSH CUT WIRE

Before cutting the wire, place your index finger over the tip of the wire to prevent it from flying across the room as it is being cut. Snip the wire. After cutting the wire and while you are still gripping the cutters, place your left index finger against the tool to ensure that you cannot feel the wire end.

4 MEASURE AND MARK WIRE

Once the end of the wire has been flush cut, place a ruler or measuring tape against the wire. Using the ruler, determine exactly where the wire needs to be cut, then mark it with a permanent marker.

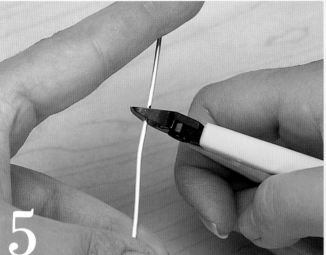

5 CUT WIRE

Holding the wire perpendicular to the flush cutter blades, as shown, cut the wire precisely at the marked point. Unless otherwise stated in the directions, wire should always be cut straight across—never angled—on both ends.

6 CLEAN WIRE

Once you cut your wire, you can remove any residual marker ink on it by simply rubbing it with 0000 steel wool. If your wire has any kinks in it, proceed to *Hammering Wire*.

TECHNIQUE 3 Hammering Wire

Two basic techniques are shown here: hammering wire with a hard-plastic mallet to straighten, harden and remove any kinks from the material, and using a chasing hammer to flatten the wire. Hammering with a hard-plastic mallet will strengthen the wire as it hardens, while flattening the wire with a chasing hammer actually weakens the material and makes it more brittle.

To hold the hammer or mallet correctly, pretend you're holding a tennis racket, preparing to hit the ball over the net. Wrap your thumb and all four fingers around the handle, as shown,

resisting the temptation to place your index finger on top.

1 HAMMER OUT KINKS

Work out any kinks in the wire with a plastic-headed mallet. Use the mallet to pound the wire on a steel bench block, which rests on a shock-absorbing leather pillow.

2 FLATTEN WIRE

When instructed to do so, use a chasing hammer to flatten the wire. Pound the wire on a steel bench block resting on a leather pillow until the wire is flat.

The secret to making a tight, perfect spiral is to be patient and make tiny movements, bending the wire ⅛" (3mm) at a time. It's easy—just follow the steps outlined below.

1 FLATTEN WIRE END
Place one end of the wire on a steel bench block and tap it several times with a chasing hammer until flat.

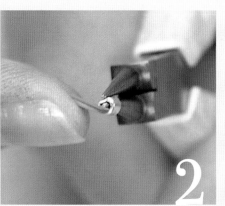

2 GRIP WIRE
Grip the flattened end of the wire in the tips of your round-nose pliers. Bend the wire by rolling your wrist forward, away from your body while gripping the wire tightly in the tips of your pliers. Bend the wire until it forms a small *U* shape. This is the beginning of your spiral.

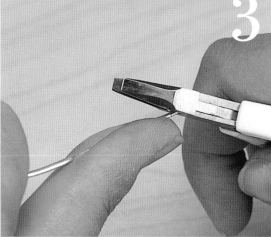

3 BEND THE WIRE
Place the *U* shape sideways in the back of the flat-nose pliers, and use your left thumb to press the straight wire against the beginning spiral, conforming to its shape.

4 CONTINUE THE SPIRAL
Open the tool, slide the spiral back around so the straight wire is facing you again, and repeat bending the wire around the spiral in small increments. You want to keep the spiral tight, as shown.

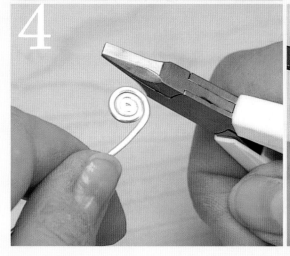

5 REMOVE TOOL MARKS
If your tool leaves any marks, you can simply file them away. Be sure to move the file in one direction only.

Making Jump Rings

A jump ring is essentially a wire circle with an opening. This basic jewelry-making component has many uses. Jump rings are used to dangle beads, charms and other items off a necklace or bracelet chain, and can be used to make the chain itself as well. While you can purchase ready-made jump rings from catalogs and bead stores, it makes good economic sense to create your own. And remember, by making your own jump rings, you control their size, weight, color and shape.

First, create coils using a nail

The first step in making jump rings is to coil the wire. This can be done by wrapping the wire around a long nail.

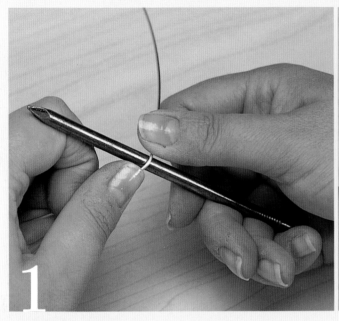

1 START COIL
Begin a wire coil by pressing the middle of the wire length against the nail with your left thumb, as shown. Rotate the nail forward, coiling the wire tightly as you go.

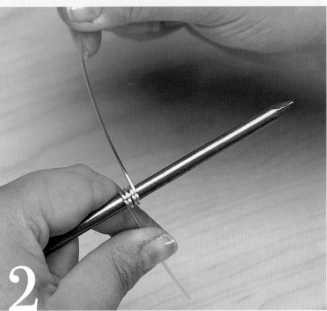

2 COIL WIRE
Continue coiling the wire tightly around the nail.

Note that wire becomes stiffer the longer you  work with it. This is called *work-hardening*. As you manipulate the wire, electrical charges are sent up the length of the wire, causing it to work-harden.

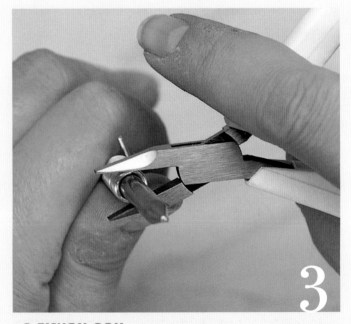

3 FINISH COIL
Continue coiling until you reach the end of the wire. Use pliers to curl the very end of the wire length onto the nail, completing the coil.

18

... or create coils with round-nose pliers

Instead of using a nail to coil the wire, you can use a pair of round-nose pliers.

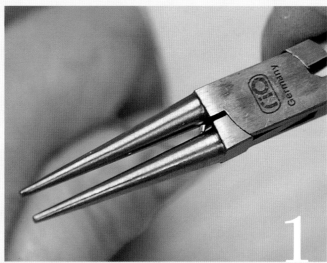

1 GRIP WIRE IN BACK OF PLIERS
Grip one flush-cut end of wire firmly in the back of the round-nose pliers.

2 START COIL
Begin a wire coil by pressing your left thumb against the wire as shown and then rotate your right hand forward, away from your body. Continue rotating your hand until the wire is wrapped around once. Open the jaws of the pliers, rotate your hand back toward your body and re-close the pliers.

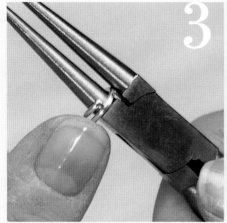

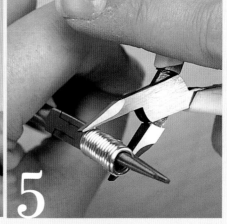

3 CREATE FIRST COIL
Rotate your hand forward again and the short end of the wire should come into view. To make coils of equal size, bring the long end of the wire to the right of the short end and continue to rotate your hand forward.

4 CONTINUE COIL
Open the tool as before and rotate your hand back toward your body. Then, close the tool on the wire and rotate your hand forward again. Continue this process until you have coiled a sufficient length of wire to make several jump rings.

5 FINISH COIL
To finish coiling a length of wire, use flat- or chain-nose pliers to press down the very end of the wire so that it conforms to the coil shape. The wire end will become stiff due to work-hardening (see *Tip*, page 18).

Then, proceed to make jump rings

After the wire has been coiled, fashion the individual coils into jump rings.

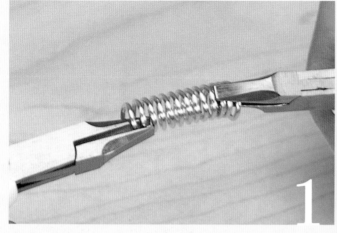

1 PULL COILS APART
Prior to cutting your jump rings apart, use your flat- and chain-nose pliers to separate the rings. This will prevent you from inadvertently snapping off the pointed ends of your flush cutters while cutting jump rings that are coiled too close together.

2 FLUSH CUT WIRE END
Once the coils are separated, flush cut one end of the wire.

3 CUT FIRST JUMP RING
Line up the flush cutters with the wire end that you just cut in step 2. Cut off a single jump ring.

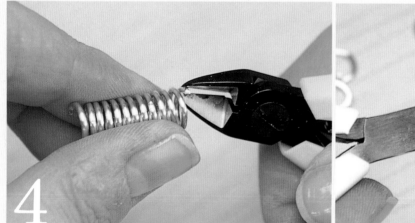

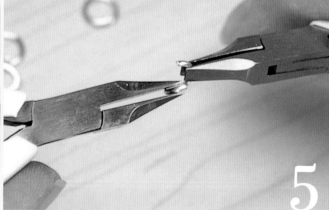

4 MAKE A FLUSH CUT
After you cut off your first jump ring, the end of the coiled wire will be wedge-shaped. Cut off the wedge shape by flipping the cutters over in your right hand and flush cutting the coiled wire end. This little bit of wire may be discarded. Cut off another jump ring. Repeat this process of flush cutting the wire and cutting off the jump rings until you have used up the entire coil.

5 CONDITION JUMP RINGS
Condition your jump rings by gripping each end of the ring with a pair of pliers and wiggling the ends back and forth until they click together.

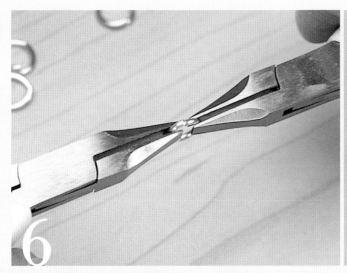

6 SHAPE JUMP RINGS

When you are finished conditioning the jump rings, each ring will be slightly twisted so the ends may not meet. Use the tips of your pliers to gently work the ends of the jump ring back together. Take your time with this process, as beautifully formed jump rings have great impact on finished jewelry pieces.

7 FINISH JUMP RINGS

If necessary, finish each jump ring by gently pressing the wire ends down in the tips of your pliers. When finished, the two ends of the ring should meet. You want your jump rings to be seamless, like a perfect circle.

9 FLATTEN JUMP RINGS

If you want to flatten the jump rings, lightly tap them with a chasing hammer on a steel bench block. If you choose to do this, the ends of the jump ring will come apart; recondition the ends to work them back together.

8 HAMMER JUMP RINGS

Use a hard-plastic mallet and steel bench block to hammer and further work-harden your jump rings.

It's handy to have a supply of perfect jump rings at your fingertips when you're working on a project. I recommend conditioning and completely closing all the jump rings before putting them in your jewelry box.

tip

When assembling jewelry, you will be attaching bead dangles and other components to jump rings. Before doing this, it is important to know how to open and close the jump rings correctly.

To avoid distorting your jump rings, always open them side to side, as shown.

Close them the same way—side to side.

See how attempting to open a jump ring by pulling it straight apart ruins it forever? You certainly won't make that mistake twice!

TECHNIQUE 6 Making Twisted-Wire Jump Rings

You can sometimes find twisted-wire jump rings available to purchase, but they're rare and expensive. It's really easy to make your own by using an electric drill with a keyless chuck. Two effective methods for twisting wire are offered on these pages.

First, twist a single length of wire
The first step in making these decorative jump rings is to twist the wire. This can be done with one length of wire, bent in half.

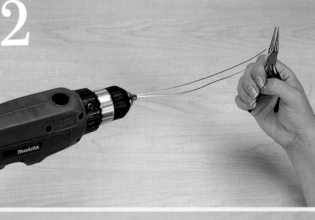

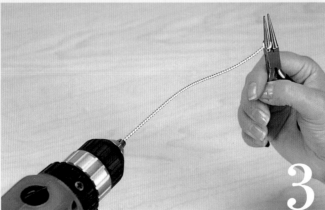

1 BEND WIRE
Flush cut one length of wire, then bend the length in half.

2 SECURE WIRE IN DRILL
Loosen the drill chuck and insert the two wire ends. Tighten the chuck to secure the wire. Holding the drill up, grip the bent end of the wire securely with pliers.

3 TWIST WIRE
Turn the drill on and let the wire twist until the wire breaks off; it will usually break right at the chuck of the drill.

... or twist two equal lengths of wire

Alternatively, you can twist two separate lengths of wire cut to the same size. Use this method if you are twisting two different kinds of wire together (see *Tip*, below).

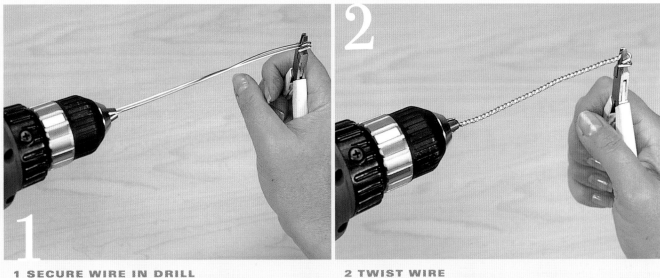

1 SECURE WIRE IN DRILL

Cut two pieces of wire the same length. Insert the wire ends into the drill chuck, then tighten the chuck. Grip the two remaining wire ends with your pliers and curl the wire into a loop around the plier jaws.

2 TWIST WIRE

Gripping the ends of the wire firmly with the pliers, turn the drill on and allow the wire to twist until it breaks off.

Then, proceed to make jump rings

After twisting the wire, you can coil it and cut it as usual to make jump rings.

Twisted-wire jump rings can be made with silver and copper or silver and gold wire. These combinations offer a completely different look, which can be accented by the types of beads or pearls you use with them. You can also twist wire of different gauges together to create yet another look.

1 MAKE AND CUT JUMP RINGS

Follow the standard procedure for making jump rings, as described on pages 18–21.

2 HAMMER JUMP RINGS

After conditioning and closing the jump rings, use a chasing hammer to pound each side of the rings on a steel bench block.

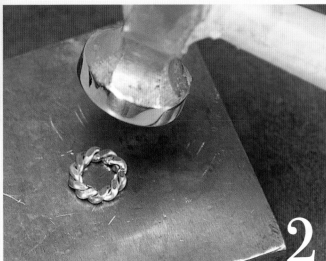

Making a Simple Eye Pin

An eye pin is a piece of wire with a loop formation, usually located at one end (or both ends) of the wire. Eye pins are commonly used for connecting beads or jewelry findings. They're easy to make in just a few steps.

1 FLUSH CUT WIRE

Flush cut a piece of wire on either end to the desired length. If you will be putting a bead on the eye pin, make sure that your wire piece is long enough and thin enough to accommodate the bead.

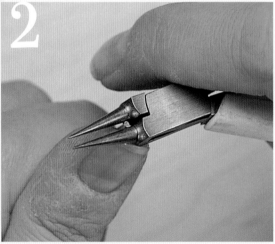

2 GRIP WIRE

Place one end of the wire in the back of the round-nose pliers, as shown. While gripping the wire tightly with the pliers, feel for any protruding wire with your left index finger. You should not be able to feel the wire end.

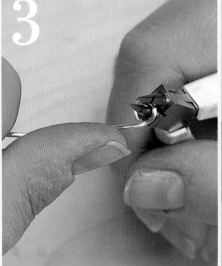

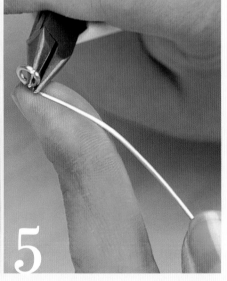

3 BEND WIRE

Gripping the wire tightly in the back of the pliers, brace your left thumb against the straight wire. Roll your wrist forward until the wire end touches the straight wire.

4 GRIP WITH CHAIN-NOSE PLIERS

Remove the round-nose pliers from the wire. Grip the wire loop in the tips of the chain-nose pliers, as shown.

5 BREAK NECK

Bracing the straight wire against your left index finger, push your right wrist forward to create a sharp bend in the wire. This is known as *breaking the neck* at the bottom of the eye pin.

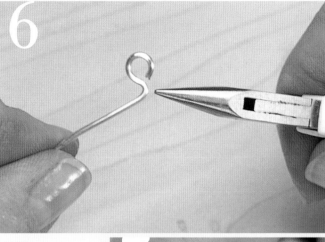

6 CHECK FOR CURVE

After breaking the neck, you should have a little curve right below the loop, as shown.

7 SHAPE EYE PIN

Reinsert the round-nose pliers into the loop and press your thumb into the neck of the eye pin. Use your thumb to bring the bent neck directly below the eye pin. Roll your right wrist forward a tiny bit to shape it.

8 STRAIGHTEN WIRE

When complete, your wire should have a lollipop formation. If the wire length below the eye pin is crooked, press it gently with a pair of pliers to straighten it out.

To add a bead to an eye pin

You can add a bead to an eye pin, following the directions below. For a more detailed description of making a bead connector, see pages 36–37.

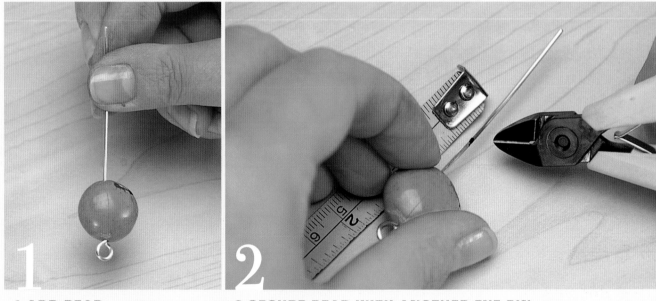

1 ADD BEAD

Slide the bead onto the wire and push it all the way down to the eye pin.

2 SECURE BEAD WITH ANOTHER EYE PIN

Place a ruler next to the remaining wire, then measure ½" (13mm) from the top of the bead, as shown. Cut the wire at the ½" (13mm) point. Grip the remaining wire with your pliers and make an eye pin to secure the bead.

Note: The measurement of the remaining wire may vary depending on the size of the desired eye pin; if using extra-large pliers, leave 1" (25mm).

Coiling one piece of wire around another to make coil-wrapped beads is a very important basic technique that you can master with ease. Just follow the steps outlined below, and soon you'll be coiling wire like an expert.

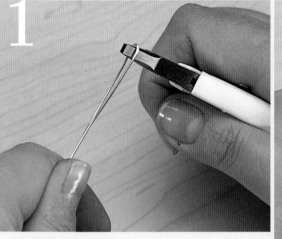

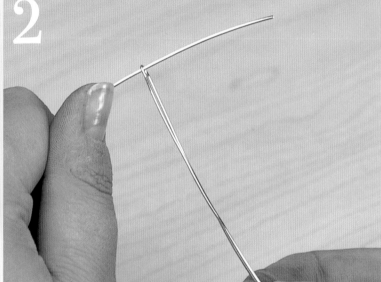

1 BEND WIRE

To begin coiling fine-gauge (20-, 22- or 24-gauge) wire, cut off a length of wire and bend it in half with flat-nose pliers. (The photo above shows an 18" [46cm] length of 20-gauge wire.)

2 SLIP BENT WIRE ONTO MANDREL WIRE

Slip the bent wire onto a 6" (15cm) 18-gauge mandrel wire (see *Tip*, below).

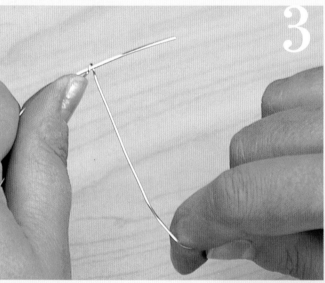

3 MAKE HAND CRANK

Bring one end of the bent 20-gauge wire around the 18-gauge mandrel wire. To make a hand crank, bend the coiling wire about 2" (5cm) away from the mandrel wire.

4 CONTINUE WRAPPING

Continue wrapping the 20-gauge wire away from your body and around the mandrel wire, gripping the wire tightly and pulling out as you wrap to create a tight coil. Each coil should lie snug against the one preceding it.

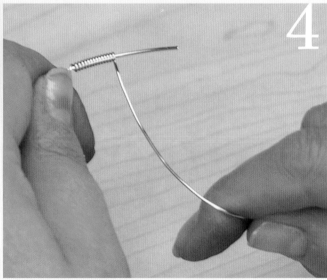

tip

A mandrel wire, not to be confused with a ring mandrel or neck mandrel, is simply a length of wire around which you wrap another piece of wire to create a coil.

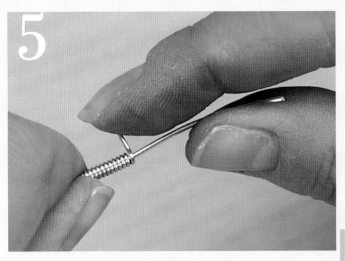

5 FINISH WRAPPING
Continue coiling the wire until you get to the end of the 20-gauge length. When you reach the end of the wire, wrap it around the mandrel wire as tightly as possible.

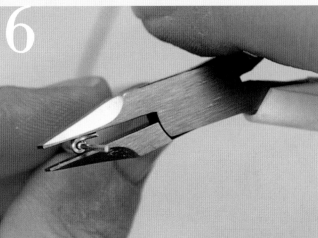

6 FINISH END OF WIRE
The last ¼" (6mm) or so of wire will be stiff due to work-hardening. If the end of the wire is too stiff to bend with your fingers, use pliers to press it around the mandrel wire. At this point, you have coiled half of the fine-gauge wire.

When wrapping the wire, keep the wire tight and flush. Do not bring it around at an angle, as shown below (lower left). If an angle forms, just unwrap the wire and rewrap it correctly. If you have trouble holding onto the wire, use shelf liner to grip it more securely, as shown below (lower right).

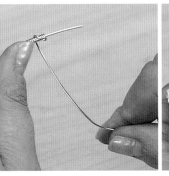

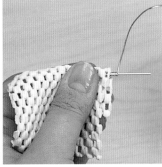

7 PULL DOWN COIL
Pull the coiled wire nearly to end of the mandrel wire length. Coil the opposite half of the fine-gauge wire. Start by unwrapping the coil just a bit, and then rewrap the wire following steps 3 to 6.

Making a Single-Coiled Bead Wrap

Coiled bead wraps present new design options and allow you to apply ancient techniques to contemporary jewelry. To make a single-coiled bead wrap, make a basic coil as instructed on pages 26–27, then move on to the following steps.

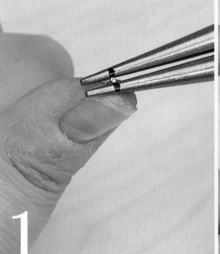

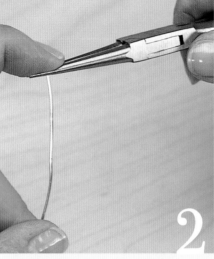

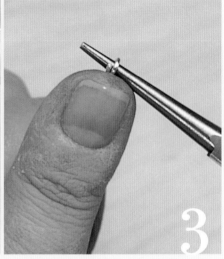

1 MARK PLIERS

Before beginning, mark the pliers with a permanent marker about one-third of the way down from the tips (see *Tip*, below). Grip the end of the 18-gauge mandrel wire that holds the coiled wire. Hold the wire in the pliers at the point marked.

2 CHECK WIRE BEFORE CUTTING

While gripping the wire, use your left index finger to make sure that you cannot feel the wire protruding beyond the plier jaws.

3 BEGIN WRAPPING WIRE

Begin a coil by pressing your left thumb against the wire, as shown, then rotate your right hand forward, away from your body. Continue rotating your hand until the wire is wrapped around once. Open the jaws of the pliers, rotate your hand back toward your body and re-close the pliers.

4 PUSH COIL DOWN TO MEET PLIERS

Wrap the wire around the pliers three times. Place the pliers on your work surface, then grip the top of the mandrel wire with another pair of pliers. While holding the mandrel wire vertical, push the coiled wire down the mandrel wire until it meets the jaws of the pliers.

When you use pliers to make several identical wire components for a jewelry project, use a permanent marker to mark the tool precisely where the wire needs to be wrapped. Use this mark as a guide each time you make a component to ensure consistency.

tip

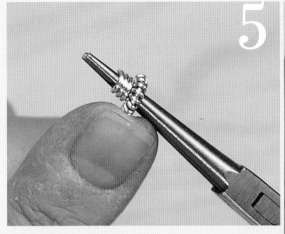

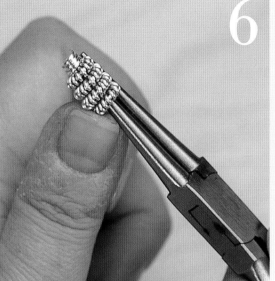

5 BEGIN WRAPPING COILED WIRE

Begin wrapping the coiled wire around the jaw of the pliers, pressing your left thumb against the wire, as shown, and then rotating your right hand forward, away from your body.

6 CONTINUE WRAPPING COILED WIRE

Continue wrapping the coiled wire around the jaw of the pliers until you have completed four wraps. The first and last wrap should be tighter and smaller than the inner two.

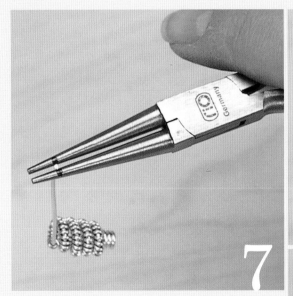

7 GRIP REMAINING LENGTH

Remove the wrapped wire from the pliers. Grip the remaining length of wire, or the *naked wire*, at the marker point so that the wire and the coil form an *L* shape.

8 WRAP REMAINING WIRE

Wrap the remaining length of wire around the pliers to make three coils.

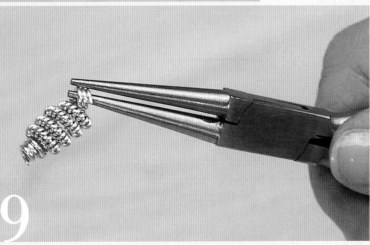

9 BEND COILED END

Slide the coiled wire off the pliers. With the tip of the pliers, lightly grip the end that you just coiled in step 8 and begin to bend it inward.

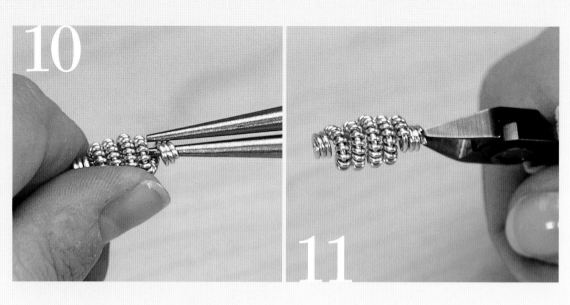

10 POSITION COILED END
Position the coiled end to mirror the opposite end, then tuck it in.

11 TRIM COILED END
Finish by trimming the tip of the coiled end, as needed.

TECHNIQUE 10 Making a Double-Coiled Bead Wrap

Making a double-coiled bead wrap involves wrapping fine-gauge wire onto a larger-gauge base wire, and then wrapping this coil-wrapped wire onto another, still larger-gauge wire. It may sound complicated, but it's really quite easy. Once you get started, you'll find many ways to apply double-coiled wire wraps to your favorite beads.

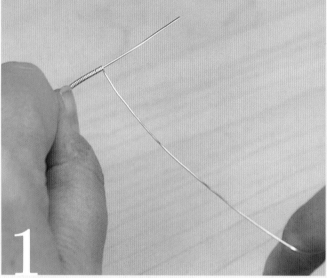

1 MAKE BASIC COIL
Following the technique for making a basic coil on pages 26–27, coil 36" (91cm) of 24-gauge wire onto a 12" (30cm) mandrel of 22-gauge wire, as shown. Bring the coil to the center of the mandrel wire, then bend the wire in half.

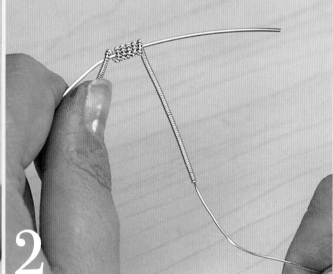

2 WRAP COILED WIRE AROUND ANOTHER LENGTH OF WIRE
Slip the bent wire onto a 9" (23cm) mandrel of 18-gauge wire. Begin wrapping the coiled part of the 12" (30cm) wire onto the mandrel wire.

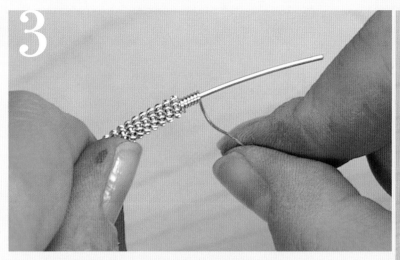

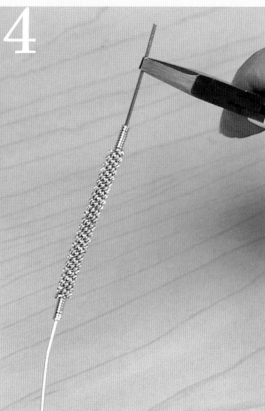

3 CONTINUE WRAPPING NAKED WIRE

When you get to the naked wire (the uncoiled ends of the 12" [30cm] length), continue wrapping.

4 FINISH WRAPPING WIRE

Wrap the entire 12" (30cm) length of wire. When you're finished, the coiled wire should be in the center, with naked wire on either end.

5 COIL WIRE

Grip one end of the wrapped wire with the pliers. Begin wrapping the naked wire around the jaw of the pliers, pressing your left thumb against the wire, and then rotate your right hand forward, away from your body. Continue rotating the pliers to coil the wire.

6 COMPLETE COIL

Coil the wire around the pliers until there is no more wire left. Coil the remaining naked wire to mirror the opposite end.

7 TUCK IN ENDS

Tuck in the end of the wire to complete the bead wrap.

Making a Wrapped Eye Pin Link

Eye pin links are versatile jewelry components that can be made in lengths varying from 1" (3cm) to about 4" (10cm) in gauges from 18 to 12. Try wrapping your links with 24-, 22- or 20-gauge round wire.

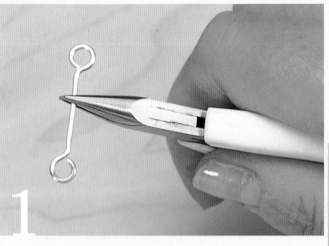

1 MAKE SAMPLE EYE PIN

Make an eye pin on each end of a length of wire, sized to suit your specific project. Refer to the technique on pages 24–25 if you need instruction on making a simple eye pin.

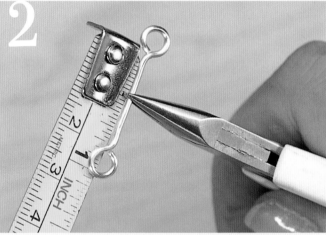

2 MEASURE WIRE

Hold a ruler right next to the wire. Measure only the straight wire between the two eye pins.

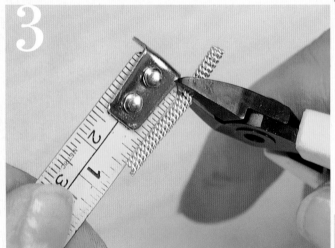

3 COIL AND CUT WIRE

Coil a length of wire, following the technique on pages 26–27. Cut the coiled wire to the exact measurement taken in step 2.

4 TRIM COILED WIRE

Flush cut the sharp end of the coiled wire.

 tip

Make long lengths of coiled wire ahead of time to keep in your jewelry toolkit. When you are working on a project that calls for coiled wire, you'll be prepared. Simply cut lengths of it as needed and you're ready to go.

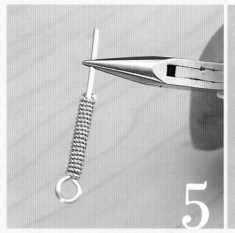

5 MAKE EYE PIN AND ADD COILED WIRE

Flush cut several lengths of wire to match the length used to make the sample eye pin in step 1. Fashion an eye pin on one end of each length, then slide the coiled wire onto the open ends of the eye pin lengths.

6 SECURE COIL WITH SECOND EYE PIN

Make an eye pin on the straight end of the wire to secure the coil, then turn the eye pin so that it is diagonally opposed to the other eye pin.

7 BREAK NECK

Break the neck of the eye pin with the chain-nose pliers.

8 FINISH EYE PIN

Reinsert the round-nose pliers and roll your wrist forward to shape and finish the eye pin.

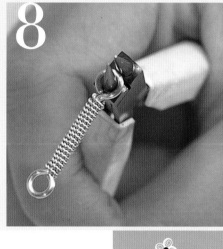

Keep your jewelry toolkit stocked with wrapped eye pin links by making several in a variety of sizes. Pictured below are links ranging from 2¹⁄₂" (6cm) to 1¹⁄₂" (4cm).

tip

9 FLATTEN EYE PINS

Use a chasing hammer and steel bench block to flatten the eye pins on each end.

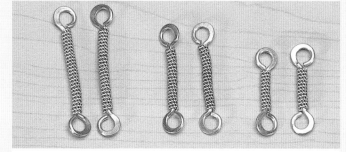

Making a Bead Dangle With a Single Eye Pin

You'll find many creative uses for bead dangles, especially these delicate dangles made with single eye pins.

1 ADD BEAD(S) TO HEAD PIN

Slip your bead(s) onto a head pin. (For this bead dangle, I have chosen a decorative head pin and a pearl.) Grip the wire with the round-nose pliers about ½" (13mm) above the bead. Create an eye pin by bringing the wire around the pliers once to make one full loop.

34

2 BREAK NECK

Break the neck of the eye pin with the chain-nose pliers.

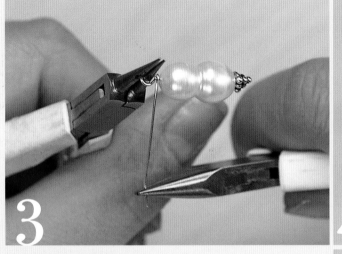

3 WRAP TAIL AROUND NECK

Reinsert the round-nose pliers where they were originally placed and, with your left hand, grip the pliers to hold the dangle steady. With your right hand, use another pair of pliers to grip the tail of the wire and wrap it snugly around the neck of the eye pin.

4 BEGIN SPIRALING TAIL

Grip the end of the wire in the tip of the round-nose pliers and begin to spiral the wire in. (For more instruction, see *Making a Spiral*, page 17.)

5 FINISH SPIRAL

Use the chain-nose pliers to continue spiraling the wire. When the spiral is finished, use the tip of the tool to tuck it against the bead, as shown.

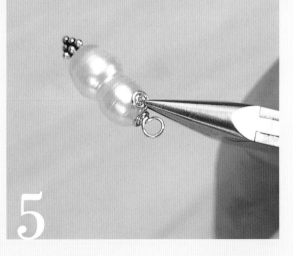

Making a Bead Dangle With a Double Eye Pin

Double eye-pin bead dangles are especially secure and useful for many applications, from earring dangles to components suitable for charm bracelets and necklaces.

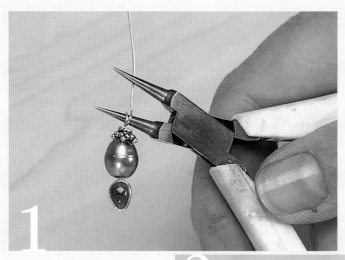

1 ADD BEADS TO HEAD PIN AND WRAP WIRE

Slip your bead(s) onto a head pin. (For this bead dangle, I have chosen a decorative head pin, a dark pearl and a silver bead cap.) Hold the head pin in the center of the round-nose pliers about ½" (13mm) above the bead cap. Loop the wire around the lower jaw of the pliers, as shown.

2 WRAP WIRE ONCE MORE

Wrap the wire around the pliers one more time so that the wire is wrapped in two full loops around the the pliers, forming an eye pin.

3 BREAK NECK

Insert the top jaw of the chain-nose pliers into the loop and grip the wire. Break the neck of the eye pin.

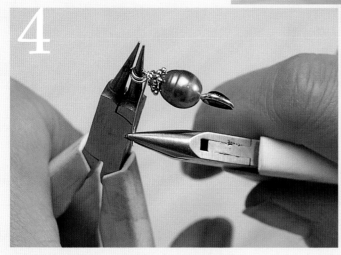

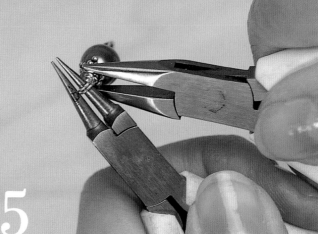

4 WRAP TAIL AROUND NECK

Reinsert the round-nose pliers where they were originally placed and, with your left hand, grip the pliers to hold the dangle steady. With your right hand, grip the tail of the wire and wrap it around the neck of the eye pin.

5 FINISH WRAPPING

Continue wrapping the tail around the neck. Use the chain-nose pliers to press the very end of the wire against the bead so it is not protruding.

Making a Bead Connector

Bead connectors are used in bracelets, anklets and necklaces to connect jump rings, beads, wire links and other jewelry components. They can be fashioned with beads in any shape or size, but take care to use plenty of wire when making connectors with large beads.

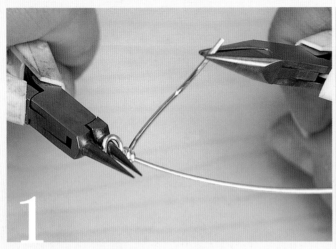

1 MAKE EYE PIN
Use the round-nose pliers to create an eye pin from a long piece of flush-cut wire. Break the neck of the eye pin against your finger, then wrap the tail wire around the neck of the loop twice.

2 ADD BEAD
Slide your bead onto the straight end of the wire.

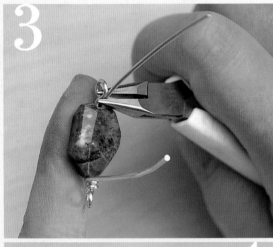

3 SECURE BEAD WITH EYE PIN
Secure the bead on the wire by fashioning another eye pin. Break the neck of the eye pin against your finger.

4 WRAP TAIL
Wrap the tail wire around the neck of the loop two or three times to mirror the opposite end.

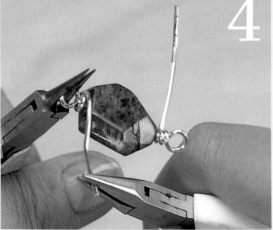

5 CUT AND FLATTEN ENDS
Flush cut the ends of the wire to the desired length, usually about 1½" (4cm). Flatten the remaining ends with a chasing hammer on a steel bench block.
Note: Heavier gauge wire, such as 18- or 16-gauge, should be flattened. Thinner wire, however, does not require flattening.

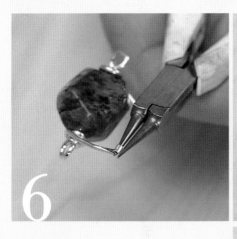

6 BEGIN SPIRALING TAIL
Grip the flattened end of the wire in the tip of the round-nose pliers and begin to spiral the wire in. (For more instruction, see *Making a Spiral,* page 17.)

7 FINISH SPIRAL
Use the chain-nose pliers to continue spiraling the wire. When the spiral is finished, use the tip of the tool to tuck it against the bead, as shown.

8 HAMMER EYE PINS
With a chasing hammer, very lightly hammer the eye pins to give the piece a finished look.

TECHNIQUE 15 Making a Coiled-Wire Bead Wrap

Plain beads are easily accented with coiled-wire bead wraps, and this technique is also a great ploy for showing off a special focal bead. Practice making coiled-wire bead wraps until you've mastered the technique, then feel free to alter your wire measurements to fit larger or smaller beads.

1 MAKE SINGLE-COILED WRAP
Make an eye pin from a length of wire, then set it aside. (For more instruction, see *Making a Simple Eye Pin,* pages 24–25.) Make a single-coiled bead wrap, as described on pages 28–30. Once finished, loosen the wrap in the middle by twisting it counterclockwise, as shown.

2 ADD COILED WRAP AND BEAD TO EYE PIN
Place one end of the coiled wrap on the wire length of the eye pin and slide it down to the neck of the eye pin. Next, slide a bead onto the wire, as shown.

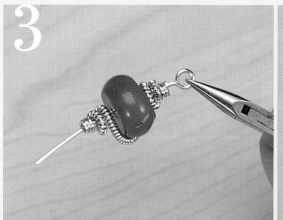

3 WRAP COIL AROUND BEAD

Wrap the loosened center of the coiled wrap around the bead, then slide what remains of the coiled wrap onto the wire.

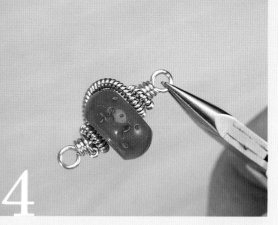

4 SECURE BEAD WITH EYE PIN

Flush cut the remaining wire, leaving enough to make an eye pin. Fashion an eye pin on the open end to secure the coiled bead. The cut ends of the two eye pins should be diagonally opposed to each other.

5 FLATTEN EYE PINS

For a finished look, flatten each eye pin with a chasing hammer on a steel bench block.

TECHNIQUE 16 Making a Double-Coiled Wire Bead Wrap

The double-coiled wire can also be used to embellish a bead. It has the same look as a single-coiled wire bead wrap, but offers a fancier, more intricate appearance.

1 MAKE DOUBLE-COILED BEAD WRAP

Make a double-coiled bead wrap, as shown on pages 30–31. Loosen the wrap in the center.

2 PLACE BEAD ON EYE PIN AND WRAP

Make an eye pin. Slide one end of the coiled bead wrap down to the neck of the eye pin, followed by a bead. Wrap the loosened center of the coiled wrap around the bead, then slide what remains of the coiled wrap onto the wire. Fashion an eye pin on the open end of the wire to secure the coiled bead. The cut ends of the two eye pins should be diagonally opposed to each other. For a finished look, flatten each eye pin with a chasing hammer on a steel bench block.

Caged beads add a touch of elegance to any jewelry design, and they have the additional benefit of showing off your beads without covering them up with too much wire. Most beads can be caged with an 8" (20cm) length of 16-gauge round wire, but if you are using very small beads in your design, shorten the wire to 6" (15cm) or so.

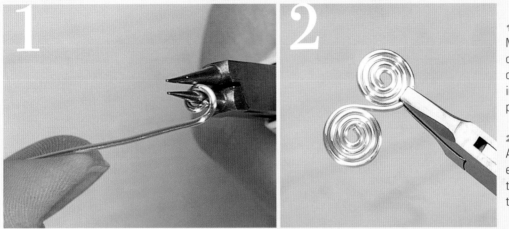

1 START SPIRAL

Measure and flush cut 8" (20cm) of 16-gauge wire. Start spiraling one end of the wire. (For more instruction, see *Making a Spiral*, page 17.)

2 CREATE *S* SHAPE

Alternate the spiraling on each end, working little by little so that the spiraled ends are equal and the length of wire looks like an *S*.

3 FORM DOMES

Push up through the center of each spiral with your round-nose pliers to create two little domes.

4 BEND IN HALF AND SPREAD COILS

Bend the piece in half, so that the dome bases are facing each other. Spread the coils apart a bit to form a small oval "cage."

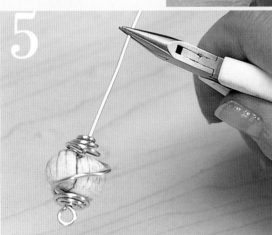

5 CAGE BEAD

Use your pliers to open the cage in the center, just wide enough to insert a bead. Place the bead inside the cage so that the center spiral wraps around it. Make a simple eye pin, then run the wire length through the caged bead.

6 SECURE CAGED BEAD WITH EYE PIN

Cut the wire, leaving slightly more than ½" (13mm) at the end. Form another eye pin to secure the caged bead. If desired, bend the wire as shown to tighten the cage around the bead.

Easy links are used to make necklace and bracelet chains, but they can also be used singly for connection to an *S* clasp. Make small easy links with fine-gauge wire for a chain, or make large, chunky links using heavy-gauge wire.

1 MAKE EYE PIN
Flush cut a 1½" (4cm) length of 16-gauge wire. Make an eye pin at one end of the wire. (For more instruction, see *Making a Simple Eye Pin,* pages 24–25.)

2 LOOP TAIL
Place the tail of the eye pin at the back of the extra-long round-nose pliers, then roll the wire all the way around to form a loop that is perpendicular to the eye pin, as shown.

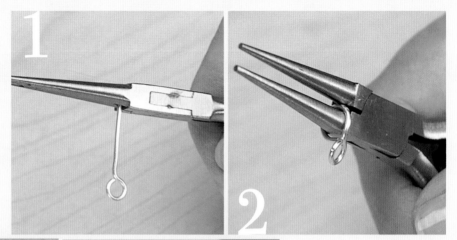

40

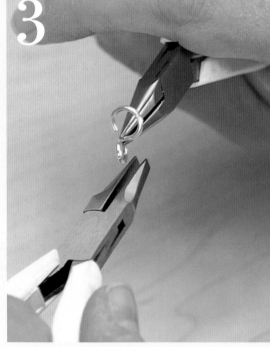

4 REPOSITION LOOP
Reinsert the extra-long round-nose pliers where they were originally placed on the loop, then bring the neck forward, back to its original position.

3 BREAK NECK OF LOOP
Holding the small eye pin with the flat-nose pliers, bend the loop back with the round-nose pliers to break its neck.

5 FLATTEN LOOP
If desired, give the link a finished look by flattening the larger loop with a chasing hammer on a steel bench block.

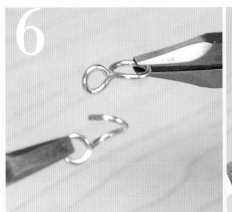

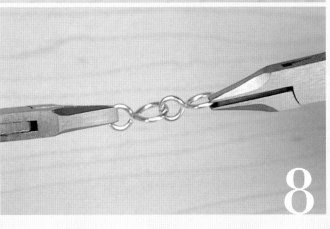

6 MAKE MORE LINKS

Proceed to make several more identical easy links until you have enough for the jewelry piece you are making. Open up the larger loop of one link as you would open up a jump ring. (For instruction on opening and closing jump rings, see *Tip*, page 22.)

7 JOIN LINKS

Run the open loop through the smaller eye pin of another link.

8 SECURE LINKS

Close the loop to secure the pair. Continue joining links in this manner until you have reached the necessary length for your jewelry piece.

TECHNIQUE 19 **Making and Joining *S* Links**

S links are elegant in shape and design, and they present many opportunities for dangling small beads and charms for bracelets and necklaces. Try making short *S* links for bracelets and longer *S* links for necklaces. Join them with doubled jump rings for a classic look.

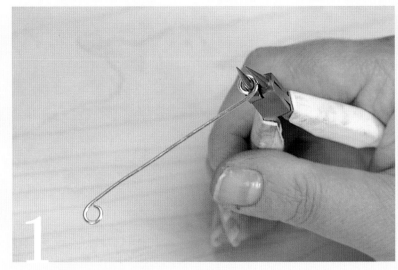

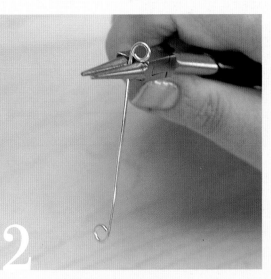

1 MAKE LOOPS

Flush cut a 3½" (9cm) length of wire. Place one end of the wire in the back of your round-nose pliers and grip the pliers firmly with your right hand. Roll your right hand forward, bracing the wire with your left thumb, to create a *P* shape. Bring the loop all the way around until it touches the straight wire. Repeat on the other end of the wire, but form the *P* in the opposite direction.

2 START LARGE LOOP

At the back of the round-nose pliers, grip the wire right under one of the loops, with the rounded *P* shape facing your body, as shown.

3 CREATE LARGE LOOP

In one fluid motion, roll your right wrist forward, pushing the *P* shape around until it touches the straight wire. Repeat with the *P* shape at the other end.

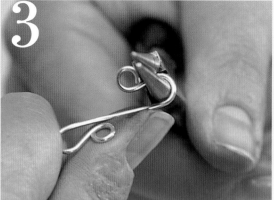

4 FINISH LINK AND MAKE MORE

When finished, you should have an *S* link shaped like the one pictured above. Proceed to make several more identical *S* links until you have enough for the jewelry piece you are making.

5 FLATTEN LINK

Manipulation of the wire will probably cause you to create a slightly crooked link with a few kinks in it. Eliminate the kinks by using a hard-plastic mallet to tap it sharply on a steel bench block. If desired, give the link a finished look by flattening the large loops with a chasing hammer (see *Tips*, below).

If the traditional *S* link is too long to make a comfortable bracelet, alter its size by using 3¼" (8cm) of wire instead of 3½" (9cm). This small change can make a big difference in the appearance of your bracelet.

Keep in mind that flattening the wire causes the links to open a bit and also lengthens the link by as much as ¼" (6mm).

6 JOIN LINKS

Open two jump rings and run them through the large loops of two *S* links, placed end to end. (For instruction on opening and closing jump rings, see *Tip*, page 22.)

7 SECURE LINKS

Close the jump rings to secure the pair. Continue joining *S* links in this manner until you have reached the necessary length for your jewelry piece.

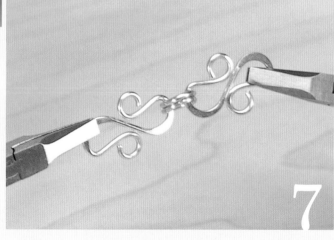

Making a Circle Link

Circle links are very easy to make, and when linked together in a simple, repeated pattern, they ensure a successful design. Try making your circle links using sterling silver, copper or gold-filled wire.

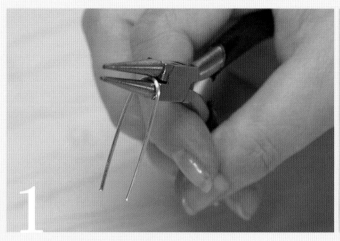

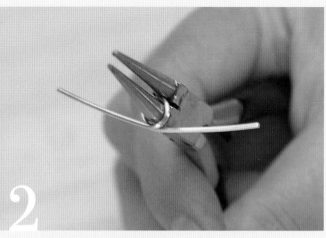

1 CUT AND BEND WIRE

Flush cut 3" (8cm) of 16-gauge wire. Grip the center of the wire, placing it in the back of the extra-long round-nose pliers. Bend the wire in half, bending down the wire on either side of the pliers.

2 FORM CENTER LOOP

Continue bending one half of the wire until you form a *P* shape, then repeat with the other half. When finished, you should have a single loop in the center of the wire, as shown.

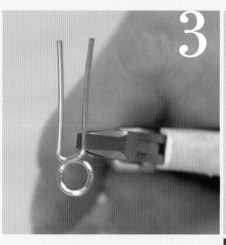

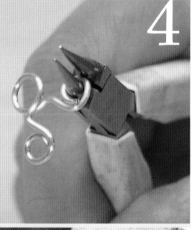

3 BEND WIRE

Use the flat-nose pliers to bend up one half of the wire, directly under the loop. Repeat with the other half so that both tails are parallel, as shown. If the tails are not equal in length, flush cut one to make them equal.

4 FORM EYE PINS

Use the round-nose pliers to create an eye pin with each wire tail.

5 FLATTEN LOOP

Flatten the center loop with a chasing hammer on a steel bench block. Several links can be joined to one another with jump rings.

Making a Heart Link

So romantic! So versatile, too—the heart link can be made in different sizes with various wire gauges for completely different looks, and whether linked side by side or point to point, its quiet elegance adds flair to your jewelry designs.

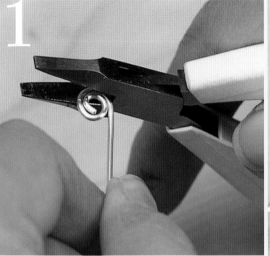

44

1 CREATE SPIRAL
Flush cut a 3" (8cm) length of wire. Grip the wire in the center of the round-nose pliers, then wrap the wire around to begin a loop, stopping before the end of the wire touches the length. Use the pliers to spiral the wire tightly one time around the loop, trying to keep the spiral round rather than teardrop-shaped. Continue spiraling the wire in the back of the flat-nose pliers, as shown.

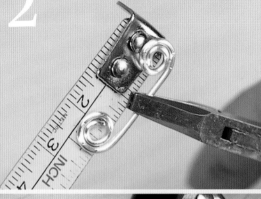

2 SPIRAL OTHER END
Repeat with the other end, spiraling the wire so that the two spirals curl in toward each other. Continue spiraling each end, little by little, until the entire piece measures 1" (25mm) from end to end.

3 FIND CENTER POINT
Use a ruler to find the center point of the link, then mark the point on the wire with a permanent marker.

4 BEND LINK TO FORM HEART SHAPE
Grip the wire with the flat-nose pliers precisely at the center point. Bend each side of the link in, bracing the center with your thumb, to form a heart shape.

5 FLATTEN LINK
Flatten the link by tapping it lightly with a chasing hammer on a steel bench block. Several links can be joined to one another with jump rings.

Putting a bead dangle on a heart link

A heart link can be "dressed up" simply by adding a bead dangle to the wire before you spiral it closed.

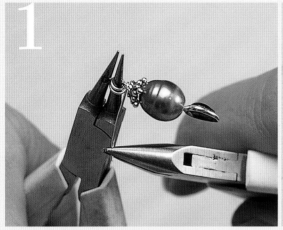

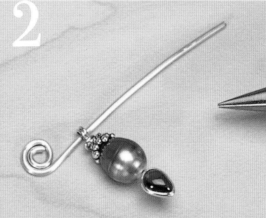

2 SPIRAL ONE END AND ADD BEAD DANGLE
Flush cut a 3" (8cm) length of wire. Spiral one end of the wire, as in step 1 on the previous page. Slip the bead dangle onto the straight end of the wire.

1 MAKE BEAD DANGLE
Make a bead dangle with a double eye pin. (For instructions, see *Making a Bead Dangle With a Double Eye Pin,* page 35.)

3 SECURE THE BEAD
Secure the bead by spiraling the other end of the heart link. Spiral the two ends until the link measures 1" (25mm) from end to end. Then, bend the two sides of the link toward each other at the center point, forming a heart shape.

tip

Never hammer where two wires cross or they'll break.

4 FLATTEN LINK CAREFULLY
Flatten the link by lightly hammering it with a chasing hammer. Hold onto the bead dangle as you hammer, keeping it off the steel bench block (see *Tip*, at right).

TECHNIQUE 22 Making a Hook-and-Eye Clasp

The hook-and-eye clasp is practical and easy to make in just a few minutes. Use it on necklaces, bracelets and anklets for a simple closure.

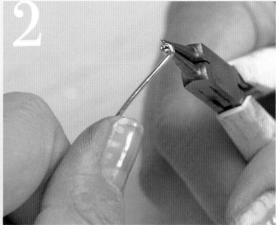

2 FORM SMALL LOOP

Wrap the flattened end of the wire around the tip of the round-nose pliers, forming a small loop.

1 FLATTEN ONE END OF WIRE

Begin the hook by flush cutting a 2" (5cm) length of 16-gauge wire. Flatten one end by pounding it with a chasing hammer on a steel bench block.

3 GRIP WIRE

Grip the wire about ½" (13mm) below the loop, placing the wire at the back of the extra-long round-nose pliers with the loop facing you.

4 FORM HOOK

Wrap the wire forward until the bottom of the small loop is touching the length, as shown, to create the hook.

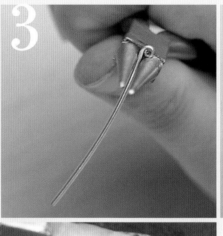

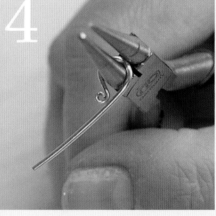

5 FLATTEN HOOK

Flatten the back of the hook with a chasing hammer on a steel bench block.

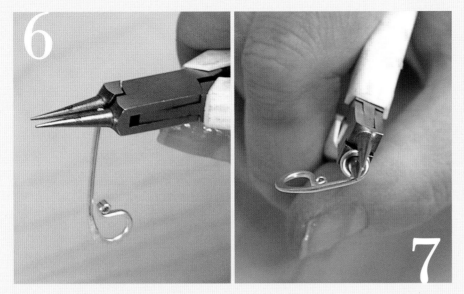

6 GRIP TIP OF WIRE
Grip the wire with round-nose pliers, placing the tip of the straight wire in the back of the pliers.

7 FORM LOOP
With the hook facing either to the left or to the right, but not facing toward you, wrap the wire forward until the end is touching the length, forming an eye pin.

8 BREAK NECK
Break the neck of the eye pin with the chain-nose pliers.

9 BEND EYE PIN
Reinsert the round-nose pliers into the eye pin, then bend it back to form a lollipop shape, with the eye pin perpendicular to the hook.

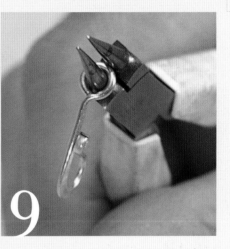

10 FINISH HOOK
As a finishing touch, press the eye pin in the flat-nose pliers, then gently pull up ever so slightly to give the hook a nice curve.

11 MAKE EASY LINK
Make the eye of the clasp by following the directions for making easy links, page 40.

12 ATTACH HOOK AND EASY LINK
Attach the hook to one end of the necklace, as shown. On the other end, attach the easy link.

Variation of a hook-and-eye clasp

This eye is made a little differently, but it's a nice variation, and one you may find useful.

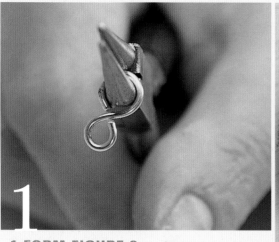

1 FORM FIGURE 8
Flush cut 1½" (4cm) of 16-gauge wire. Make a small loop with the small round-nose pliers and a larger loop with the extra-large round-nose pliers to make a figure 8, as shown.

2 FLATTEN WIRE
Flatten the wire with a chasing hammer. When you are ready to attach the clasp, secure the hook to one end of the necklace and the figure-8 eye to the other end.

Making a Hook Clasp for Linked Jewelry

Sometimes it's necessary to fasten a hook clasp directly onto a linked jewelry piece, especially on a delicate bracelet. Follow the steps below to make a wire hook. When you're finished making your jewelry piece, attach the hook to one end by wrapping the long ends of the wire around the last link.

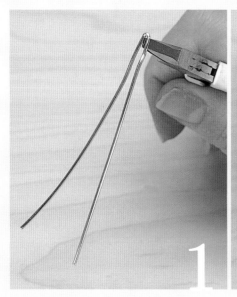

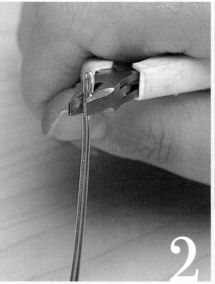

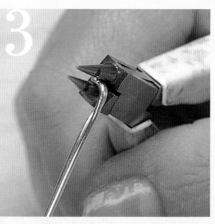

3 BEND WIRE AT TIP
With the round-nose pliers, grip the tip of the bent end of the wire. Roll your wrist forward to create a small bend in the wire right at the tip.

1 CUT AND BEND WIRE
Flush cut a length of wire. (The length and the gauge of the wire will depend on the size and gauge of the jewelry.) Bend the wire in half with the flat-nose pliers.

2 PRESS TWO ENDS TOGETHER
Use the flat-nose pliers to press the two ends of the wire together firmly, directly under the bent center.

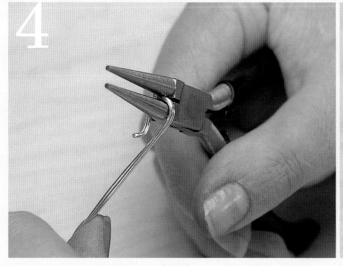

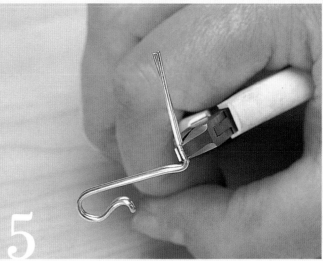

4 CREATE HOOK
Grip the wire at the back of the extra-long round-nose pliers, about ¼" (6mm) below the bent tip, which should be facing you. Bend the tip up and over into a hook.

5 BEND WIRE ENDS
Make sure that the two tails of straight wire are equal; if not, trim the ends as needed. Measure 1" (25mm) from the end of the tails. Grip the tails together at the 1" (25mm) point with the flat-head pliers, then bend them both up at a 90 degree angle, as shown. Attach the clasp by wrapping each tail around the last link of the bracelet or necklace.

Making an *S* Clasp

S clasps can be purchased in bead stores and general craft shops, but it's much more fun to make them yourself. And by making your own *S* clasp, you control its size, shape and color. Use shorter lengths of wire to make tiny *S* clasps for delicate jewelry, and longer lengths of wire to make larger clasps for bolder, chunkier pieces.

1 CUT WIRE AND FLATTEN ONE END
Flush cut 4½" (11cm) of 14-gauge wire. Flatten one end of the wire with a chasing hammer on a steel bench block.

2 FORM SMALL LOOP
Wrap the flattened end of the wire around the tip of the round-nose pliers, forming a small loop.

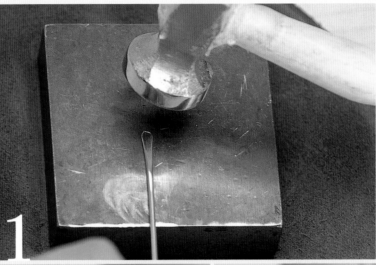

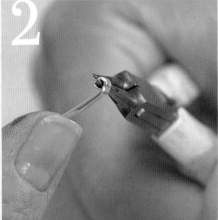

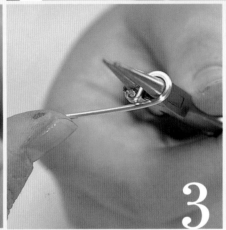

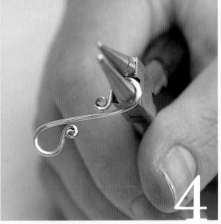

3 FORM LARGE LOOP
Grip the wire about ½" (13mm) below the loop, placing the wire at the back of the extra-long round-nose pliers with the loop facing you. Wrap the wire forward until the bottom of the small loop is touching the length, as shown.

4 REPEAT ON OTHER END
Repeat on the other end of the wire to form an *S* shape.

5 FLATTEN ROUNDED ENDS
Flatten the rounded ends of the clasp with a chasing hammer. To attach the clasp to a necklace, open the loops sideways and attach the clasp to jump rings or easy links on the necklace. Close the loops to secure.

Making an *S* Clasp With a Bead

Adding a small bead or pearl to an *S* clasp will complement your jewelry piece.

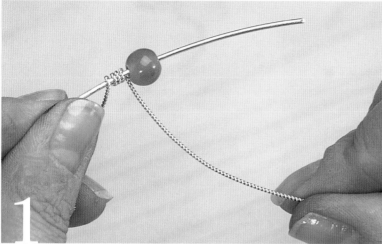

1 WRAP WIRE AND ADD BEAD

Flush cut 3" (8cm) of wire. Flush cut at least 5" (13cm) of a finer-gauge wire, then twist it with a drill. Wrap the length of twisted wire around the heavier-gauge wire at least three times, then slip a bead onto the wire.

2 FINISH WRAPPING

Run the twisted wire over the bead, then continue wrapping the wire to mirror the other side. The bead should be secure between the two wrapped sides. When you're finished wrapping, use the flat-nose pliers to grip and then slightly crimp the wire around the bead, as shown.

3 TRIM TWISTED WIRE

With flush cutters, trim the unwrapped ends of the twisted wire.

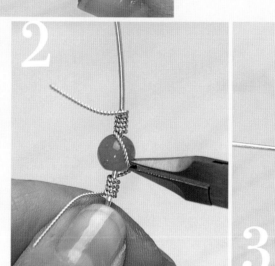

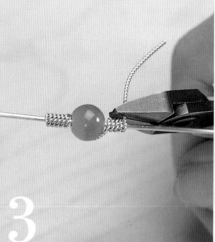

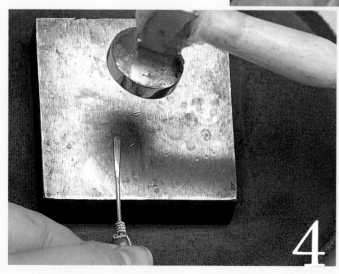

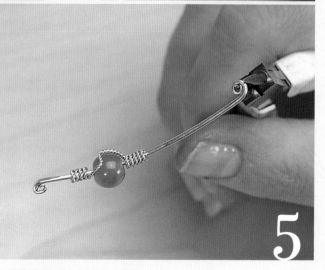

4 FLATTEN BOTH ENDS

Flatten both ends of the naked wire with a chasing hammer on a steel bench block.

5 FORM SMALL LOOPS

Wrap each flattened end of the wire around the tip of the round-nose pliers, forming a small loop on either side.

6 FORM LARGE LOOPS

Grip the wire about ½" (13mm) below one loop, placing the wire at the back of the extra-long round-nose pliers with the loop facing you. Wrap the wire forward until the bottom of the small loop is touching the length. Repeat on the other side to form an *S* shape.

7 FLATTEN ENDS

Flatten the rounded ends of the clasp with a chasing hammer. To attach the clasp to a necklace, open the loops sideways and attach the clasp to jump rings or easy links on the necklace. Close the loops to secure.

TECHNIQUE **26** Making a "Big Hook" Clasp

This big, bold hook clasp makes a beautiful closure for *Beaded Bangles* (pages 68–69) and *Arty Chokers* (pages 84–87). Practice by making it with 16-gauge wire first. When you have mastered this clasp, make another one with 14-gauge wire.

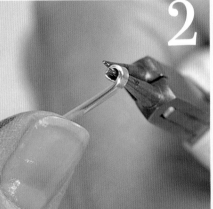

2 FORM SMALL LOOP

Wrap one flattened end of the wire around the tip of the round-nose pliers, forming a small loop.

1 CUT WIRE AND FLATTEN ONE END

Flush cut 4½" (11cm) of 14-gauge wire. Flatten both ends of the wire with a chasing hammer on a steel bench block.

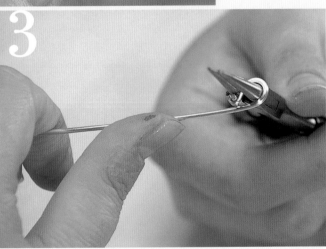

3 FORM LARGE LOOP

Grip the wire about ½" (13mm) below the loop, placing the wire at the back of the extra-long round-nose pliers with the loop facing you. Wrap the wire forward until the bottom of the small loop is touching the length, as shown.

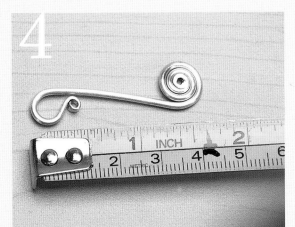

4 SPIRAL OTHER END
Start a small spiral on the other flattened end of the wire. (For instructions, see *Making a Spiral,* page 17.) Continue spiraling the wire until the entire clasp measures 1⅝" (4cm) from end to end.

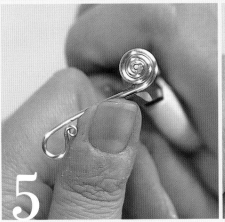

5 BEND WIRE
With the flat-nose pliers, grip the wire at the base of the spiral. Place the thumb of your free hand against the center length of wire and bend it up.

6 CONTINUE BENDING WIRE
Continue bending the wire with your thumb until a point forms below the spiral.

7 BEND SPIRAL
Grip the spiral between the flat-nose pliers, then bend the spiral around to fit inside the curve of the clasp end, as shown.

8 FLATTEN CLASP END
Flatten the clasp end with a chasing hammer on a steel bench block. To attach the clasp to a bangle, open the eye pin on one end of the bangle, drop the clasp onto it, then close the eye pin to secure.

Making a Pendant Suspender

Sometimes after selecting a beautiful pendant, you realize that it was made to dangle from a neck wire, not from the linked necklace you have already designed. No need to worry—this problem is easily solved with a pendant suspender.

1 CUT AND PLACE WIRE
Flush cut a 3" (8cm) length of 16-gauge wire. Run the wire through the pendant bale.

2 BEND THE ENDS
Center the pendant on the wire, then bend up the two equal ends of wire.

3 MAKE EYE PINS
Use the extra-long round-nose pliers to make an eye pin on either side of the bale.

4 HAMMER SUSPENDER
Hammer the suspender with a hard-plastic mallet on a steel bench block. Flatten each eye pin with a chasing hammer, taking care not to hammer the pendant.

5 RESHAPE SUSPENDER
When you hammer the suspender, a gap will often form between the two eye pins. If this happens, reinsert the extra-long round-nose pliers into each eye pin and close the gap.

Pendant dependents are beautiful links that assist in creating long, *Y*-shaped necklaces. Try suspending several strands of bead dangles in a tassel formation from your pendant dependent.

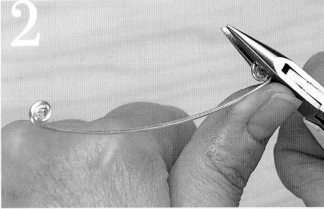

2 SPIRAL ENDS

Use the round-nose pliers to spiral each end toward the center. Spiral the ends alternately, little by little, until the piece is just about 3" (8cm) long from end to end.

1 CUT AND FLATTEN WIRE

Flush cut a 5" (13cm) length of 16-gauge wire. Flatten each end with a chasing hammer on a steel bench block.

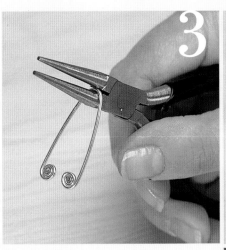

3 BEND IN HALF

Grip the center of the wire at the back of the extra-long round-nose pliers. Bend the wire in half, pushing each side down so that the spirals are facing each other.

4 FORM LOOPS

Place one spiraled end of the wire in the back of the extra-long round-nose pliers, with the spiral facing you. Brace your left thumb on top of the wire and roll your right wrist forward, bringing the spiral up and over until it touches the straight wire. Repeat with the other spiraled end. There should now be three loops.

5 FLATTEN WIRE

Flatten the three rounded loops on the pendant dependent with a chasing hammer.

Sharpening and Filing Wire to a Point

When making wire brooches or pins, it's necessary to file one end of the wire to a smooth, sharp point. Follow the steps outlined below for making successful pins that won't snag your clothing.

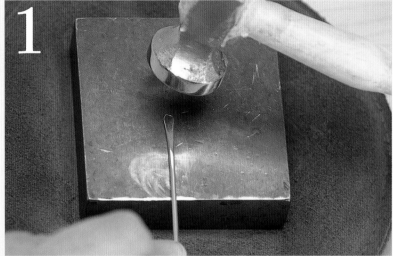

1 FLATTEN WIRE
Flatten the end of the wire with a chasing hammer.

2 CUT END TO POINT
Cut the flattened wire to a point, cutting each side of the wire at an angle, as shown, rather than perpendicular.

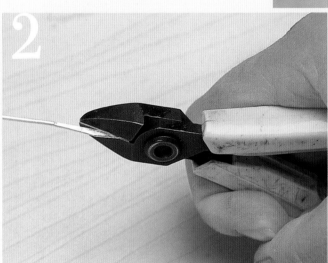

When sharpening the point, use your files and your 0000 steel wool quite vigorously. The goal is to create the smoothest point possible. This will prevent the wire from snagging on fine-weave clothing.

 tip

3 FILE POINT
File the point, rubbing a flat file in one direction to eliminate the rough edge.

4 POLISH EDGE
Polish the edge well with 0000 steel wool.

Making Charms From Leftover Wire

If, at the end of your projects, you have scraps of wire remaining, don't throw them away unless they're under 1" (25mm) long. Leftovers can be used to make small jump rings or little charms. Hammer them and shape the pieces into spirals, squiggles, geometric shapes or anything that pleases you. Save your charms for inclusion in a jewelry piece that calls for abstract design elements.

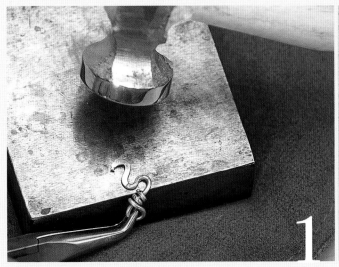

1 SHAPE WIRE SCRAPS
Use various methods described in the *Techniques* section to shape small accent pieces from wire scraps. Flatten the pieces as desired with a chasing hammer.

2 STORE AND USE ACCENT PIECES
Store the accent pieces in your bead box. Use the miscellaneous accent pieces as charms and embellishments for your jewelry projects.

TECHNIQUE **31** # Artificially Aging Jewelry

Use liver of sulfur to artificially age your jewelry, giving it the look of a valuable ancient artifact in just minutes! The steps outlined below demonstrate how to "antique" your jewelry and polish it to a high shine. You can apply this method safely to silver, copper or brass (but not gold) jewelry made with any type of beads or pearls, with these exceptions: bone or ivory beads, or polymer clay. Be sure to work in a well-ventilated area, and never add liver of sulfur to boiling water.

2 DIP JEWELRY IN SOLUTION
Use pliers to drop jewelry into the solution until it is fully submerged. Allow the jewelry to sit in the solution for a few minutes, and then remove it with a plastic implement, such as tongs.

1 MIX LIVER-OF-SULFUR SOLUTION
Drop a small chunk of liver of sulfur into a small- or medium-size bowl of hot (not boiling) water. Agitate the water until the liver of sulfur is fully dissolved.

3 RINSE JEWELRY

After removing the jewelry from the solution, place it in a bowl of tepid water to rinse. The water will turn yellow.

4 DRY JEWELRY

Once the jewelry has been rinsed, place it on a few layers of paper towel. Thoroughly pat the jewelry dry with another paper towel. At this stage, I always leave my jewelry out overnight to dry completely.

Always use a tool to place the jewelry in and out of the solution. Plastic tongs work best, but you can also use pliers or even a chopstick, as shown at left. Avoid allowing the solution to touch your skin. If it touches your skin, the solution will create a stinging sensation and will cause your skin to smell like sulfur.

tip

5 POLISH WITH STEEL WOOL

When the jewelry is completely dry, lay a sheet of paper towel over your work surface. Working over the paper towel, polish the jewelry with 0000 steel wool. For faster results, polish in one direction only.

Note: 0000 steel wool is safe to use with beaded jewelry; it will not even scratch beads.

6 BRUSH OUT STEEL WOOL

Use a brass brush to remove any bits of steel wool that may have gotten into the crevices of the jewelry.

7 POLISH JEWELRY WITH CLOTH

Using firm pressure, polish the piece with a jewelry polishing cloth, such as a Sunshine cloth. Continue polishing as desired. When finished, store the polishing cloth in an air-tight plastic storage bag.

Sharilyn's Tips for Jewelry Making

When it comes to designing and making jewelry, I always keep three principles in mind: creativity, wearability and durability.

Creativity is where it all starts, and, not surprisingly, this aspect of jewelry making usually provides the most enjoyment. Making an original piece of wearable art that breaks new ground in design and manufacture is a challenge, but the results of your efforts will be amply rewarded. It's fun to wear a particularly stunning piece of handmade jewelry to a social function and proudly proclaim, "I made it myself."

Wearability is my next consideration. Your jewelry might be bold and original, but is it wearable? Jewelry is often pictured and displayed on a flat surface, but this does not serve its purpose. Jewelry is made to be worn on a three-dimensional surface: the human body. Examine how a jewelry piece looks on you by standing in front of a mirror. Do those big, chunky beads on your Arty Choker make you look like Frankenstein? Is your bracelet painfully tight, or too loose to wear comfortably while typing at the computer? Is that wonderfully abstract, asymmetrical necklace making you look lopsided and weird? If so, it's time to go back and make some adjustments.

Durability is my final consideration when designing and making new jewelry pieces. It may not be a very sexy subject, but it's just as important as creativity and wearability. Picture this: You're sitting on the couch at your best friend's baby shower, and her toddler suddenly grabs hold of your handmade necklace with a jerk. Does it instantly fall apart, beads and wire links scattering across the floor? Or does it hold together because you took the time to make a durable piece of jewelry? The answer is in your hands, literally! Follow the instructions provided in the *Techniques* section, practice making durable wire links and bead wraps, and your jewelry will stand the test of time (and toddlers).

Here are a few tips to keep in mind as you begin—and, hopefully, continue—the jewelry-making process:

* Mistakes are our teachers. Let's face it, success may be our goal, but we don't learn much from it. As you start coming up with your own designs, I hope you'll embrace your mistakes instead of avoiding them. Whenever I design a successful piece of jewelry and it comes together easily, I find the process rather disappointing. How much more stimulating to run into a roadblock and have to find a way around it!

* Take care to make good jump rings. Condition your jump rings well by wiggling the wire ends together sideways until you hear them grinding together. Hammer them lightly with a hard-plastic mallet. If your jump rings were made from heavy-gauge wire such as 14 or 12, hammer them gently with a chasing hammer. If doing so opens them up slightly, close them again. Now you have some durable jump rings—the essential building blocks of most jewelry pieces.

* Take the time to make all your jewelry components well. Get in the habit of filing away rough edges, closing your eye pins securely and hammering your wire links with a hard-plastic mallet to work-harden them. The result of your efforts will be creative, wearable, durable jewelry pieces that you will be proud to wear and pass on to future generations. Your jewelry may become treasured family heirlooms worn by your granddaughters and great-granddaughters!

When it comes to designing jewelry, the journey is the destination. So go for it: Be creative, be patient, take your time, take lots of notes while you work out new designs, and embrace your mistakes. It's all part of the journey, and it starts right here.

INTRODUCTION TO THE Projects

If you're like most artists, you started on this page first, skipping through 60 pages of very important information in favor of the "eye candy" found in the following section. Well, I can hardly blame you! It's fun to look at pretty jewelry and imagine the possibilities. The projects presented here range from simple and elegant to complicated and elaborate. Beaded bangles, fibula brooches, caged-bead necklaces and bracelets, various styles of earrings and much more are offered for your enjoyment.

On the following pages, you'll find lots of easy-to-make jewelry pieces, such as the Circle Link Bracelet, Shepherd's Hook Earrings, Simple Jump Ring Bracelet and *S* Link Charm Bracelet. Then we'll challenge you with slightly more complicated pieces: the Beaded Bangle, Arty Choker, Delicate Pendant and Caged-Bead Necklace. When you've mastered the basic techniques used to make these pieces, you'll be ready for the Party Watch, Coiled-Wire Bangle, Milagro Charm Necklace and Twin-Spiral Bracelet.

Variety is important in any artistic endeavor, so I have created a jewelry collection featuring a plethora of pearls, crystals, stone beads and silver enhancements such as bead caps, charms and decorative headpins. But please don't feel compelled to make exact duplicates of the jewelry pieces shown here. Instead, let them become springboards for your imagination. For instance, a charm bracelet made with crystals would look equally stunning if fashioned from a selection of pearls or beads instead—and it would bear the stamp of its creator: you!

Beaded bangles can be assembled using just about any type of focal bead that you can imagine. I myself have made dozens, and none of them resemble the bangle shown on page 68. And as for earrings—well, don't get me started! You can make the simple shepherd's hook earring in thousands of variations, and classic hoop earrings are easily altered by the simple addition of various bead and pearl dangles or metal charms. It's easy to come up with your own unique, original designs simply by changing the beads, bead caps, headpins and other items used to create this jewelry.

As you peruse the offerings on the following pages, you will notice that each project has been "stepped out" in photography with brief text describing the steps. Experienced artists who've made lots of wire jewelry will need little more to make similar pieces. But if you haven't made much jewelry before or if you need more instruction, simply refer back to the *Techniques* section (pages 14–59), where you will be guided by text liberally illustrated with step-by-step photography. Perhaps it's not as exciting as the jewelry itself, but mastery of technique is at the heart of superior finished jewelry.

In each of the following chapters, you'll find a list of basic materials plus a list of the methods you will be using to create each jewelry piece. Page numbers for sections where the techniques have been explained in detail are also included. For instance, on page 82 you'll find *Techniques You'll Be Using* for the Simple Jump Ring Bracelet, which include cleaning and cutting wire and making bead connectors, jump rings and twisted wire jump rings, as well as the option of artificially aging your jewelry. It's a simple matter of turning to the relevant pages for instruction on these topics.

I hope you enjoy making your own creations based on the instructions offered in the *Projects* section. Have fun, and let your imagination be your guide!

Hoop Earrings

Hoop earrings are a jewelry-box staple that never goes out of style. Thousands of variations are possible with this classic design, and you can alter the look easily by adding your favorite beads and dangling charms. Found objects—anything from small game pieces to metal scraps from other jewelry projects (all edges filed smooth!)—are especially fun to place on hoop earrings. Try anything you find that has an interesting line, shape, color or texture.

TOOLS AND MATERIALS

jewelry toolkit

20-gauge round wire

various mandrels (or markers or large wooden dowels) in different sizes for forming hoops

optional:

embellishments such as beads, charms, bead dangles, predrilled found objects, coiled bead wraps and other items

liver-of-sulfur solution

TECHNIQUES YOU'LL BE USING

Cleaning and Cutting Wire (pages 15–16)

Making a Simple Eye Pin (pages 24–25)

Hammering Wire (page 16)

optional:

Making a Bead Dangle With a Single Eye Pin (page 34)

Making a Single-Coiled Bead Wrap (pages 28–30)

Making a Double-Coiled Bead Wrap (pages 30–31)

Artificially Aging Jewelry (pages 57–58)

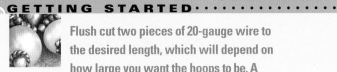

Flush cut two pieces of 20-gauge wire to the desired length, which will depend on how large you want the hoops to be. A good starting point for your first pair would be about 4" (10cm). Make sure both wire pieces are exactly the same length.

1 MAKE EYE PINS
Make an eye pin on one end of each length of wire.

2 SHAPE WIRE
At this point you will need a smooth, round mandrel; a fat marker, a ring mandrel or a large wooden dowel can be used. Wrap each wire around the mandrel to form a round or oval shape.

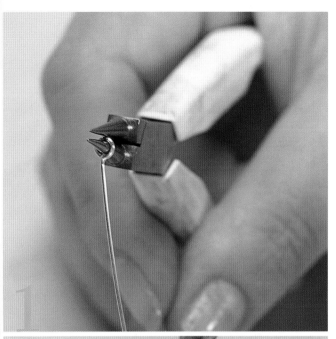

63

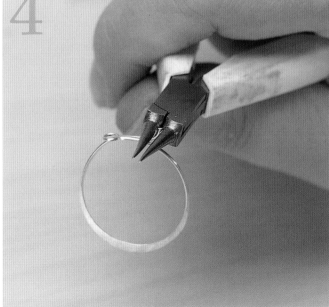

3 HAMMER WIRE
Hammer the wire with a hard-plastic mallet on a steel bench block to preserve the shape you've created. Then, flatten the bottom portion of each hoop with a chasing hammer.

4 BEND WIRE ENDS
Once you are satisfied with the design, grip the straight end of one earring wire in the middle of the round-nose pliers and bend it up in a slight curve. Repeat with the other earring wire.

It's important to file the wire end until it is very smooth because, as it passes through the pierced tissue of your earlobe, any sharp edges could create micro-tears in your skin, resulting in inflammation. Always file in one direction and, when finished, rub the wire end briskly with 0000 steel wool.

Allergic to metals? Apply a thin coat of clear nail polish to the wire where it passes through your earlobe to alleviate any problems.

Try making hoop earrings in different sizes. Giant hoops go in and out of style periodically, so once you know how to make your own it will be easy to keep pace with current trends.

5 FINISH EARRINGS

Grip the eye pin with the flat-nose pliers and bend it straight up, perpendicular to the hoop, as shown. The curved end should hook right onto the eye pin. File the end of the wire very smooth (see *Tips*, at right). Repeat for the other earring. Once assembled, you can artificially age your earrings in a liver-of-sulfur solution.

OPTIONS # Embellishments

You can add beads, charms, bead dangles, coiled-wire wraps or other items to the wire hoop. Follow steps 1 and 2, as instructed on the previous page. Then, hammer the hoops with only the hard-plastic mallet. Do not flatten the hoop. Continue with one of the following steps (or one of your own), and then finish up the earrings with steps 4 and 5. When choosing beads, charms or found objects, select lightweight items that won't drag on your earlobes.

ADD BEADS AND BEAD DANGLES

Slip your choice of beads and bead dangles directly onto the straight end of the wire.

ADD COILED-BEAD WRAP

Slip a single- or double-coiled bead wrap directly onto the straight end of the wire.

Rectangle Earrings

Rectangular in shape, these earrings are made using the same general technique as the hoops. It's easy to create your own variation with ovals, squares or even triangles.

To get started, flush cut two pieces of 20-gauge wire to 4¾" (12cm). You can make the length shorter for smaller earrings or longer for larger earrings.

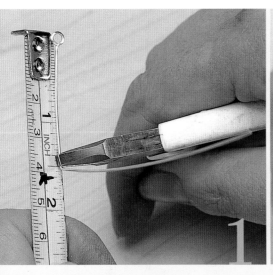

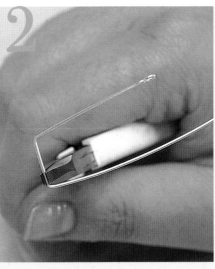

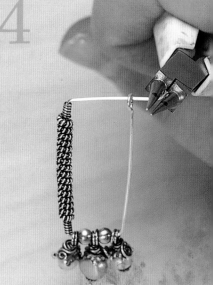

1 MAKE EYE PINS
Make an eye pin on one end of each length of wire. Hold one eye pin length alongside a ruler. At 1½" (4cm), use the flat-nose pliers to bend the wire at a 90 degree angle. Repeat for the other eye pin length.

2 BEND WIRE AGAIN
Measure ½" (13mm) from the first bend, then bend the wire back up. Hammer the wire with a hard-plastic mallet if it's crooked.

3 ADD ACCENTS
Slip a coiled-wire bead wrap, bead dangles or any other accent pieces onto the straight end of the wire. Slide the pieces into the desired position on each earring.

4 FINISH EARRINGS
Measure 1½" (4cm) of the remaining length, then bend the wire to complete the rectangle. The straight end should fit right through the eye pin. File the end of the wire very smooth. If desired, artificially age the earrings.

Circle Link Bracelet

Simplicity itself, the Circle Link Bracelet makes an elegant statement with a repeat design. If you're a beginner, this project is a good starting point, as it requires only a few fundamental techniques. The bracelet's simplicity makes it a versatile piece, appropriate to accessorize any outfit.

TOOLS AND MATERIALS

jewelry toolkit

16-gauge round wire

optional:

liver-of-sulfur solution

TECHNIQUES YOU'LL BE USING

Cleaning and Cutting Wire (pages 15–16)

Making a Circle Link (page 43)

Making Jump Rings (pages 18–22)

Making a Hook Clasp for Linked Jewelry (page 49)

optional:

Artificially Aging Jewelry (pages 57–58)

Flush cut several 3" (8cm) lengths of 16-gauge wire for 10 to 14 circle links and a 12" (31cm) length of 16-gauge wire for 20 to 24 jump rings.

1 MAKE CIRCLE LINKS

Prepare 10 to 14 circle links and flatten them with a chasing hammer. In addition to the circle links, make 20 to 24 small jump rings.

2 JOIN CIRCLE LINKS

Lay two circle links on a work table with the smaller circles facing each other. Open the jump rings and use one to connect the top of the links and another to connect the bottom. Repeat this until you have five sets of connected links. Connect the circle-link sets end to end using doubled jump rings.

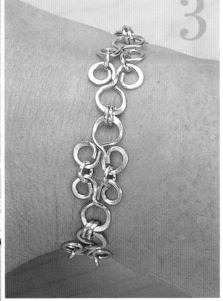

3 MAKE ADJUST-MENTS

Try the bracelet on to determine whether it needs more links or fewer to fit your wrist. Make adjustments as needed.

4 FINISH WITH CLASP

Make a hook clasp using approximately 3" (8cm) of 16-gauge round wire. Attach the hook to one end of the bracelet. Once assembled, you can artificially age your bracelet in a liver-of-sulfur solution.

Beaded Bangle

Myriad choices await you! Beaded Bangles can feature a favorite focal bead or be more simply tailored to match any outfit in your wardrobe. Try using real stone beads such as turquoise or amber, or match a handmade glass treasure with similar, less expensive beads. Consider making two different styles of bangle: large, round bangles that move freely on your wrist and smaller, elliptically-shaped bangles that fit the wrist more securely.

TOOLS AND MATERIALS

jewelry toolkit

14-gauge round wire

beads: one or more large focal beads plus several small spacer beads and coiled bead wraps, all with large holes

optional:

decorative bead caps

liver-of-sulfur solution

TECHNIQUES YOU'LL BE USING

Cleaning and Cutting Wire (pages 15–16)

Hammering Wire (page 16)

Making a Simple Eye Pin (pages 24–25)

Making a "Big Hook" Clasp (pages 52–53)

optional:

Making a Single-Coiled Bead Wrap (pages 28–30)

Artificially Aging Jewelry (pages 57–58)

Flush cut an 8½" (22cm) length of 14-gauge wire (or more or less, depending on the size of your wrist) for the bangle. Select and/or make the beads, bead caps and coiled bead wraps for your bangle. Make a "big hook" clasp from 14-gauge wire.

1 PREPARE WIRE AND ARRANGE BEADS

Hammer the 8½" (22cm) length of wire with a hard-plastic mallet to work-harden it. Slip your focal bead onto the center of the wire, then arrange the remaining beads on your work surface in the order you desire.

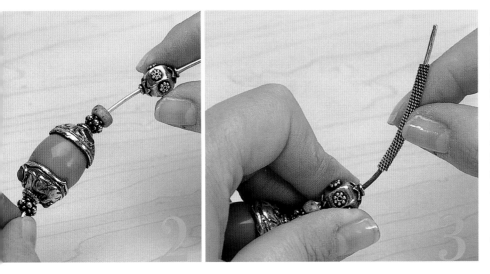

2 ADD BEADS TO WIRE

Add the beads to the wire on either side of the focal bead. When designing a bangle, it's best to start in the middle and work out toward both ends.

3 FINISH BEADING

Add the remaining beads and bead wraps, making sure to reserve 1" (25mm) of bare wire on each end for the next step.

Note: Always finish with metal beads or wrapped wire on each end of the bangle. Tension on the eye pins can cause a glass or stone bead to break.

69

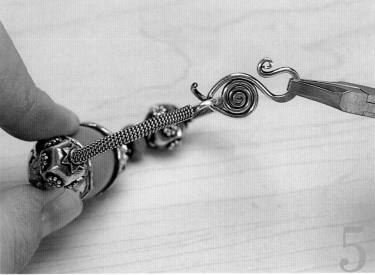

4 CREATE EYE PINS

Create an eye pin on each end of the wire on the back of the extra-long round-nose pliers. Close both eye pins securely.

5 ADD CLASP TO END OF BRACELET

Open one eye pin, attach the "big hook" clasp to it, and then close the eye pin. Once assembled, you can artificially age your bracelet in a liver-of-sulfur solution.

Classic Fibula

Based on an ancient, versatile brooch design that goes back to antiquity, fibulas can be made to suit anything in your wardrobe. There are hundreds of potential variations on the Classic Fibula. Experiment by making several brooches the same size but adorning them with different combinations of beads, charms or bead dangles.

TOOLS AND MATERIALS

jewelry toolkit

16-gauge round wire

optional:

embellishments, such as charms, bead dangles, predrilled found objects and assorted beads in various sizes

TECHNIQUES YOU'LL BE USING

Cleaning and Cutting Wire (pages 15–16)

Hammering Wire (page 16)

Sharpening and Filing Wire to a Point (page 56)

Flush cut a 12" (31cm) length of 16-gauge wire. Select and/or make an assortment of embellishment pieces, such as beads and charms, for the fibula.

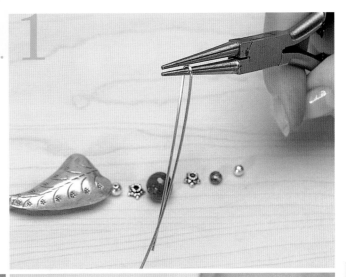

1 CUT AND BEND WIRE

Lay out beads, charms and other pieces in the desired order for your pin. At 2½" (6cm) from one end of the 12" (31cm) length, grip the wire with extra-long round-nose pliers, placing it about one-third the way from the tip of the pliers. Use the pliers to bend the wire back, as shown.

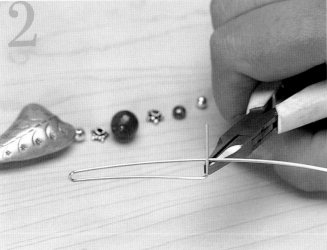

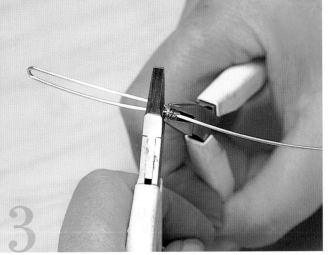

2 BEND WIRE AGAIN

On the shorter half of the wire, bend the wire up ¾" (2mm) from the end.

3 WRAP WIRE

Grip the wire with flat-nose pliers to hold it steady, then use the chain-nose pliers to wrap the short wire tail around the long end of the wire, as shown. You can flatten the end of the wire if necessary to aid wrapping. When finished, you should have a doubled-wire end.

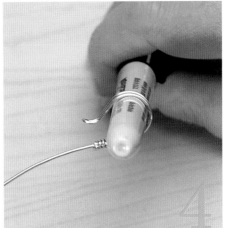

4 CREATE HOOK

Bend the tip of the doubled-wire end just slightly, and then bend the remainder of the end around a marker to form a hook shape.

5 ADD BEADS

Following the order laid out in step 1, slip your beads, charms and other pieces onto the straight end of the wire. Push them down the wire until they are flush with one another. Be sure to begin and end with a metal bead.

6 MAKE PIN SPRING

Secure the beads on the wire by adding a spring on the end. To do this, grip the wire at the end of the bead lineup on the back of the small round-nose pliers, then make one full loop around the jaw of the pliers, as shown.

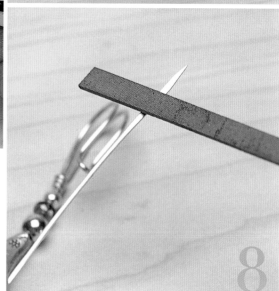

7 CUT WIRE

Cut the wire end to fit into the hook. Flatten the wire end with a chasing hammer, and then use flush cutters to trim the flattened end to a sharp point.

8 FILE END

File the point by rubbing it with a flat file in one direction, then polish it well with 0000 steel wool. When sharpening the point, use your files and steel wool quite vigorously. The goal is to create the smoothest point possible to prevent the wire from snagging on fine-weave clothing.

Classic Fibulas

With just a few beads or accent pieces, you can give every fibula you make a completely different look.

Naga Shell Fibula

Here's a nice example of a fibula pin made with a coiled-wire wrap to accent a special bead called a Naga shell.

Monochromatic Fibula

Fibulas can be made with all sorts of beads. For a classic look, use a monochromatic (one hue) color scheme such as the silver one shown here.

tips

The Classic Fibula can be made with heavier-gauge wire such as 14 or even 12, but keep in mind that such heavy wire may create large holes in fine fabrics such as silk or linen. Reserve these chunky brooches for wool sweaters or knitted scarves where large holes won't show.

Try making extra-large fibulas with 18" (46cm) of wire—or more—for wearing on a large lapel. Or, make tiny fibulas, ideal for pinning a scarf or the collar of a lightweight blouse, with 6" to 8" (15cm to 20cm) of wire.

Bead-Wrap Bracelet

In this cheerful bracelet, two distinctly different bead wraps are used to beautify and connect colorful resin beads. Consider using different beads and bead wraps as well as different wire—copper, gold or brass—to fashion your bracelet. Heavier-wire gauges used on chunky beads offer a bold, ethnic look, while 18- or 20-gauge wire and small wrapped crystal beads create a delicate appearance.

TOOLS AND MATERIALS

jewelry toolkit

16-gauge round wire and 20- or 22-gauge round wire

beads or pearls in different shapes, sizes and colors

toggle clasp

optional:

counterweight bead or charm

liver-of-sulfur solution

TECHNIQUES YOU'LL BE USING

Cleaning and Cutting Wire (pages 15–16)

Making a Caged Bead (page 39)

Making a Coiled-Wire Bead Wrap (pages 37–38)

Making a Simple Eye Pin (pages 24–25)

Making Jump Rings (pages 18–22)

optional:

Artificially Aging Jewelry (pages 57–58)

In addition, for the *Variation:*

Making and Joining Easy Links (pages 40–41)

Making a Hook-and-Eye Clasp (pages 46–48)

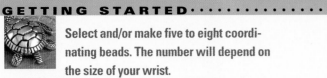

Select and/or make five to eight coordinating beads. The number will depend on the size of your wrist.

1 CREATE CAGED BEADS

Wrap some of your beads as caged beads with 16-gauge wire.

2 CREATE COILED-WIRE BEAD WRAPS

Wrap the rest of your beads as coiled-wire bead wraps with 20- or 22-gauge wire.

3 CREATE EYE PIN LINKS

With 16-gauge wire, create five to eight eye pin lengths, to be made into eye pin links for the caged beads and coiled-wire bead wraps. The length of the eye pins depends on the sizes of the beads and the length of the bracelet.

75

4 PLACE BEADS ON EYE PINS

Finish the beads by placing each on a single eye pin length, then fashion an eye pin on the opposite end to secure the bead, as shown. Flatten the eye pins slightly with a chasing hammer.

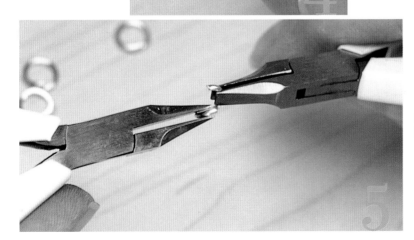

5 MAKE JUMP RINGS

Make 10 to 12 jump rings with 16-gauge wire.

6 LINK WRAPPED BEADS

Link the wrapped beads together, joining the eye pins with doubled jump rings (see step 7, below). Place the bracelet around your wrist to determine the proper length, then add or subtract wrapped beads and jump rings as needed until the bracelet fits. (The bracelet as specified in these instructions measures 8½" to 9" [22cm to 23cm].)

7 INTERLOCK JUMP RINGS IF DESIRED

If desired, attach the jump rings in an interlocking position to add a creative twist to your bracelet.

8 ADD JUMP RINGS ON ENDS

Attach small jump rings to each end of the bracelet, then add a toggle clasp.

Counterweight beads are attached near the clasp to keep it from riding up on the top of your wrist. The counter-weight bead you use needn't be very large, but it should be heavy.

tip

9 ADD COUNTERWEIGHT BEAD

If desired, add a counterweight bead onto a jump ring near the toggle (see *Tip*, at left). Once it is assembled, you can artificially age your bracelet in a liver-of-sulfur solution.

Bead-Wrap Necklace

For an easy variation, make a Bead-Wrap Necklace. Create the necklace by adding more links and beads to the jewelry, lengthening it enough to fit around your neck.

To get started, select about a dozen coordinating beads. Feel free to choose large beads with bold colors, mixing them with smaller coordinating beads.

1 WRAP AND JOIN BEADS
After you've made your selection of beads, wrap some of them as caged beads and the rest as coiled-wire bead wraps. Create eye pin lengths using 16-gauge wire. Place a wrapped bead on each length, then secure the bead with an eye pin on the opposite end. Hammer the eye pins gently with a chasing hammer. Make about 20 jump rings with 16-gauge wire and use them to link the beads in pairs, joining one coiled-bead wrap with one caged bead.

2 JOIN BEADS
Join all the beads to form a necklace. Place the necklace around your neck to determine the proper length, then add or subtract wrapped beads and jump rings as needed until it fits comfortably.

3 ATTACH EASY LINKS
Make eight to twelve easy links. Attach four to six easy links to each end of the necklace, then add a hook-and-eye clasp.

Shepherd's Hook Earrings

Combine your favorite charms or bead dangles with a simple shepherd's hook earring, and you have a five-minute piece of jewelry! These earrings provide the opportunity to show off some favorite beads or charms, so take the time to select a nice combination of beads, bead caps and decorative head pins for the bead dangles.

TOOLS AND MATERIALS

jewelry toolkit

20- or 22-gauge round wire

assorted beads, bead caps and/or pearls in various sizes and colors

optional:

liver-of-sulfur solution

TECHNIQUES YOU'LL BE USING

Cleaning and Cutting Wire (pages 15–16)

Making a Bead Dangle With a Single Eye Pin *or* a Double Eye Pin (pages 34–35)

Hammering Wire (page 16)

optional:
Artificially Aging Jewelry (pages 57–58)

In addition, for the *Variation:*

Making a Simple Eye Pin (pages 24–25)

Making a Spiral (page 17)

Select and/or make an assortment of beads, bead caps and head pins for the bead dangles. For the earrings, flush cut two lengths of 22-gauge (preferred) or 20-gauge wire, each measuring 4", 3" or 2" (10cm, 8cm or 5cm), depending on how long you want your earring wire to be.

1 MAKE BEAD DANGLES
Make two bead dangles with decorative head pins and bead caps. Once they are assembled, set them aside.

2 MAKE LOOPS
On one end of each wire length, create a single loop in the middle of the small round-nose pliers. Grip the wire directly under the loop and make another loop at the back of the extra-long round-nose pliers, as shown.

3 BEND END OF WIRE
Place the straight end of the looped wire in the back of the extra-long round-nose pliers and make a tiny bend in the last ⅛" (3mm) of the wire. Repeat with the other looped wire.

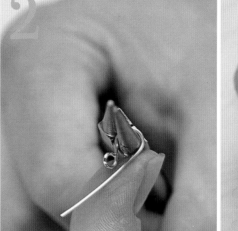

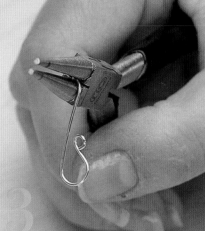

6 RESHAPE HOOK
Use pliers to pull the hook back into shape on each earring wire.

4 HAMMER WIRE
Hammer each earring wire with a hard-plastic mallet on a steel bench block.

5 FLATTEN EARRING HOOK
Use a chasing hammer to flatten the hook (rounded part) of each earring wire.

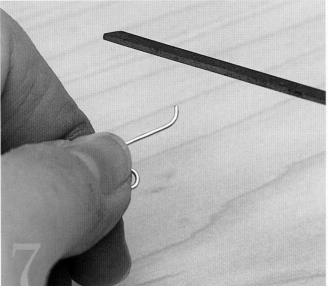

7 FILE END
File the end of the each earring wire. Be sure to file the wire in one direction only. Polish with 0000 steel wool.

8 ATTACH BEAD DANGLE
Open the earring loops sideways and slip one bead dangle onto each wire. Close the loops back up to secure. Once they are assembled, you can artificially age your earrings in a liver-of-sulfur solution.

VARIATION # Hook Earrings

This is simply a different way to make Shepherd's Hook Earrings. In this variation, you add the bead dangle *as* you are shaping the wire rather than first forming the loop and *then* attaching the dangle.

To get started, select an assortment of beads, bead caps and head pins, then make bead dangles. For the earrings, flush cut two 4" (10cm) lengths of 20-gauge wire. If you want shorter earring wires, adjust the length to 3" (8cm) or 3½" (9cm).

1 CREATE EYE PIN
Use the small round-nose pliers to grip one of the 4" (10cm) lengths of flush-cut wire 1" (25mm) from the end of the wire. While gripping the pliers, roll your wrist forward to create a loop.

2 BEND BACK WIRE TAIL
Insert the round-nose pliers into the loop as far as it will go. Place the wire on your index finger as shown, then push your right wrist forward abruptly to break the neck.

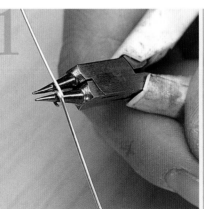

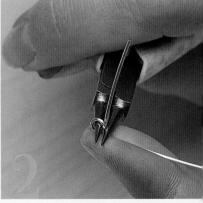

3 ADD BEAD DANDLE

Open the eye pin and place the bead dangle on it. With the pliers, squeeze the eye pin to close it back up.

4 WRAP WIRE BELOW EYE PIN

Insert the small round-nose pliers into the eye pin to hold the wire steady. Then, use the bent-nose pliers to wrap the short tail of the wire around the length three times at the base of the eye pin.

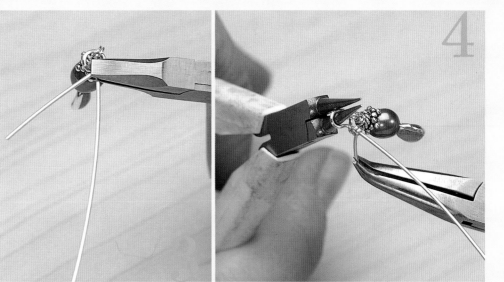

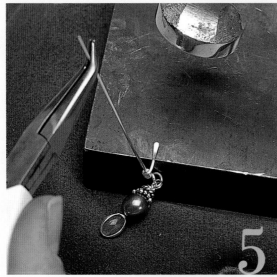

5 FLATTEN AND SPIRAL TAIL

Use a chasing hammer to flatten only the short tail remaining from the wrapped wire, as shown. Once it's flat, spiral in the wire tail and tuck it against the straight wire.

6 MAKE LOOP

Place the wire in the back of the extra-long round-nose pliers with the bead dangle hanging beneath the pliers, then bend the wire up and over the tool to create a loop.

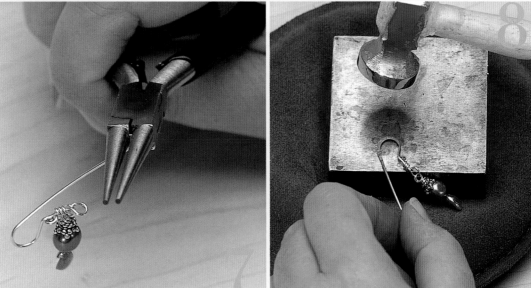

7 BEND WIRE END AND FILE

With extra-long round-nose pliers, bend the last ¼" (6mm) of wire just slightly. File the end smooth. Polish with 0000 steel wool. Make the second earring, repeating steps 1–7.

8 FLATTEN WIRE

Use a chasing hammer to flatten the rounded top of each earring wire. Once they are assembled, you can artificially age your earrings in a liver-of-sulfur solution.

Simple Jump Ring Bracelet

For this bracelet, twisted-wire jump rings are paired with bead connectors dressed with pretty bead caps. Quick and easy to put together in an afternoon, this classic design is guaranteed to please. Twisted-wire jump rings can be made with silver and copper wire or silver and gold wire—combinations that can be accented by your selection of beads or pearls.

TOOLS AND MATERIALS

jewelry toolkit

16-gauge round wire

matching beads

decorative bead caps

toggle clasp

optional:

counterweight bead or charm

liver-of-sulfur solution

TECHNIQUES YOU'LL BE USING

Cleaning and Cutting Wire (pages 15–16)

Making a Bead Connector (pages 36–37)

Making Jump Rings (pages 18–22)

Making Twisted-Wire Jump Rings (pages 22–23)

optional:

Artificially Aging Jewelry (pages 57–58)

Select six or seven beads and bead caps for bead connectors. Bead connectors can be made with silver beads, natural stone beads, crystals or pearls. If you use nonmatching beads, tie the design together by using matching bead caps.

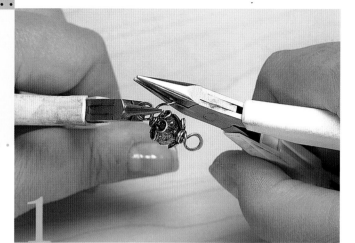

1 ASSEMBLE BEAD CONNECTORS
Make six or seven bead connectors using 16-gauge wire.

2 JOIN BEAD CONNECTORS
Use 16-gauge wire to make six to eight twisted-wire jump rings. Begin joining the bead connectors to one another with the twisted-wire jump rings.

3 MAKE BRACELET
Join all the bead connectors to form a bracelet. Place the bracelet around your wrist to determine the proper length, then add or remove connectors or jump rings until it fits.

4 ADD TOGGLE CLASP
Make at least eight small jump rings. Add four jump rings to each end of the bracelet. Connect the bar end of the toggle clasp to the last jump ring on one end and the circle end of the toggle clasp to the opposite end of the bracelet.

5 FINISH BRACELET
If desired, attach a counterweight bead and/or charm to the bar end of the bracelet. Once it is assembled, you can artificially age your bracelet in a liver-of-sulfur solution.

Arty Choker

Based on a torque design first worn by men and women of ancient civilizations, Arty Chokers may be made in different lengths to suit a variety of necklines. The perfect jewelry for showing off a favorite focal bead, these chokers are easy to make, too.

TOOLS AND MATERIALS

jewelry toolkit

12- or 14-gauge round wire

beads in various sizes, including one large focal bead

embellishments, such as bead caps, spacer beads and hanging charms

optional:

necklace mandrel

clasp

liver-of-sulfur solution

TECHNIQUES YOU'LL BE USING

Cleaning and Cutting Wire (pages 15–16)

Hammering Wire (page 16)

Making a Hook-and-Eye Clasp (pages 46–48)

optional:

Making a Single-Coiled Bead Wrap (pages 28–30)

Making a Double-Coiled Bead Wrap (pages 30–31)

Making a Coiled-Wire Bead Wrap (pages 37–38)

Making a Double-Coiled Wire Bead Wrap (page 38)

Artificially Aging Jewelry (pages 57–58)

Flush cut a 20" to 24" (51cm to 61cm) length of 12- or 14-gauge wire in sterling silver, gold, copper or brass.

1 CUT AND HAMMER WIRE

Work-harden the 20" to 24" (51cm to 61cm) length of wire by hammering it with a hard-plastic mallet. This will create a better fit around your neck.

Note: After cutting the wire, you can shape it around a necklace mandrel, then hammer the wire with a hard-plastic mallet to force it to conform to the shape of the mandrel. This optional step is quite helpful when creating a choker that fits comfortably around your neck.

2 PREPARE BEADS

Select and/or make an assortment of beads for the choker, including a central focal bead. You can wire-wrap plain beads, create coiled beads or fashion any other embellishment as desired.

3 CREATE DESIGN

Create your necklace design, arranging your beads in order on your work surface.

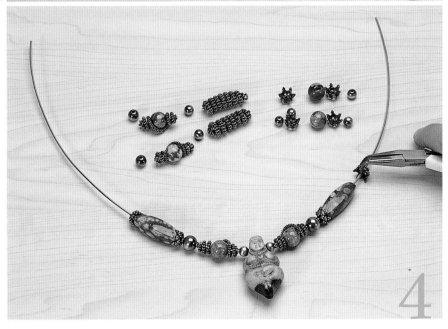

4 ASSEMBLE NECKLACE

Slide the focal bead onto the wire and bring it to the center. Place smaller beads on each side of the focal bead, following your arrangement.

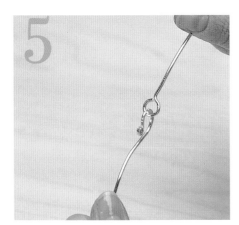

5 ADD HOOK-AND-EYE CLASP
Create a hook clasp at one end of the neck wire and an
eye pin at the opposite end.

OPTIONS **Clasps**

In addition to the hook-and-eye clasp shown in step 5 (above), there are several choices for clasps to use on Arty Chokers. These clasp options are all detailed on pages 46–53 of the *Techniques* section. Once the choker is assembled and the clasp is complete, you can artificially age your necklace in a liver-of-sulfur solution.

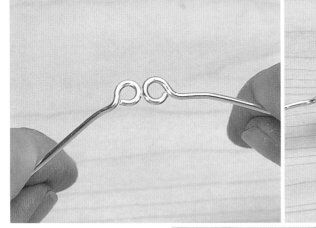

"BIG HOOK" CLASP
Create an eye pin on each end
of the neck wire, then fashion a
"big hook" clasp to hold the two
ends together.

NO CLASP
If the choker is made with
heavy wire such as 12-gauge, it
may not be necessary to use a
clasp at all, especially if you've
hammered the wire against a
necklace mandrel. In this case,
create a small eye pin on each
end of the wire to keep the
beads from slipping off.

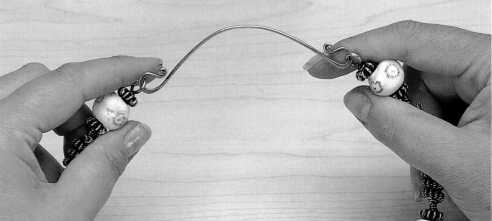

LONG DOUBLE-HOOK CLASP
You can also make a slightly shorter necklace and fashion eye pins on each end. Then, with about 6" (15cm)
of wire, create a clasp extension with a hook clasp on either end.

Designing a new Arty Choker is as simple as sliding a different combination of beads and embellishments onto another length of work-hardened wire. You can go for a quiet, subdued look or for a bold, ethnic look, like the one shown below—either way, your original design will turn heads.

Naga Shell Arty Choker

This version of the Arty Choker features a Naga-shell bead embellished with coiled wire.

tips

When selecting the gauge of wire used for this project, keep in mind that the beads you use must fit easily on the wire. Most handmade glass beads will slip onto 14-gauge or 12-gauge wire quite smoothly, but sometimes stone beads or vintage trade beads have small holes that will not accommodate heavier wire. In this case, you may be able to ream the bead holes to enlarge them, but it's always best to use wire that will fit easily through your beads. If you are really set on using beads with small holes to make an Arty Choker, try using 16-gauge wire for the neck wire—but hammer it thoroughly with a hard-plastic mallet to work-harden it and keep it from drooping.

Many types of wire-wrapping options are available for use with this necklace design. Plain beads of a medium size will benefit from being wrapped in coiled wire. Other beads with more intricate designs are best left alone, but might look even better if set off with bead caps. Another option is to create long sections of coiled wire to place on the neck wire near the back of the neck. The creative possibilities are numerous and varied, and you can make literally thousands of Arty Chokers without exhausting all of your options.

Delicate Pendant

Using this simple, classic design, you can make your own chain links to form a long necklace with bead dangles suspended from a pendant dependent. The necklace shown here was made with carnelian and Peruvian opal beads. Try making a similar necklace using pearls, crystals, handmade glass beads or any of your favorite beads or charms. This is a long necklace that fits easily over your head, but you can add an *S* clasp as a decorative feature if desired.

TOOLS AND MATERIALS

jewelry toolkit

16- and 20-gauge round wire

assorted beads

decorative bead caps

optional:

liver-of-sulfur solution

TECHNIQUES YOU'LL BE USING

Cleaning and Cutting Wire (pages 15–16)

Making a Bead Dangle With a Double Eye Pin (page 35)

Making a Bead Connector (pages 36–37)

Making and Joining Easy Links (pages 40–41)

Making a Pendant Dependent (page 55)

Making Jump Rings (pages 18–22)

optional:

Artificially Aging Jewelry (pages 57–58)

Select beads for the pendant. Make three bead dangles and six bead connectors, using bead caps as desired. Make several jump rings using a length of 20-gauge wire and several easy links using 1" (25mm) lengths of 20-gauge wire.

1 ASSEMBLE COMPONENTS

Join 30 of the easy links together, then add one bead connector to each end. Follow with four easy links and another bead connector on each end. Finish with five easy links, one bead connector and five more easy links on each end.

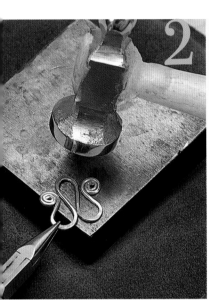

89

2 MAKE PENDANT DEPENDENT

Make a pendant dependent using a 5" (13cm) length of 16-gauge wire.

3 ATTACH PEN- DANT DEPENDENT

Open the easy links on each end of the necklace and attach the pendant dependent, as shown. Close the easy links to secure.

4 ASSEMBLE PENDANT

Create the pendant by attaching each bead dangle to several easy links. Attach the top link of each dangle to a single jump ring. The dangles should fall at different lengths, as shown.

5 FINISH NECKLACE

Add the pendant to the pendant dependent with a jump ring. Once it is assembled, you can artificially age your necklace in a liver-of-sulfur solution.

Jump Ring Charm Bracelet

Who can resist the charm of a dangly bracelet festooned with pearls, semi-precious stones and charms? Once you realize how easy they are to make, you'll want to fashion several bracelets for yourself and your loved ones. And, as you will see on page 93, expanding upon this idea to make a matching choker is easy.

TOOLS AND MATERIALS

jewelry toolkit

16-gauge round wire

matching beads and/or pearls

toggle clasp

optional:

decorative bead caps

counterweight bead or charm

liver-of-sulfur solution

TECHNIQUES YOU'LL BE USING

Cleaning and Cutting Wire (pages 15–16)

Making a Bead Dangle With a Single Eye Pin (page 34)

Making Jump Rings (pages 18–22)

Making Twisted-Wire Jump Rings (pages 22–23)

optional:

Artificially Aging Jewelry (pages 57–58)

In addition, for the *Variation:*

Making a Bead Connector (pages 36–37)

Select coordinating beads and/or pearls, and beads caps if you're using them, for the bracelet.

1 MAKE BEAD DANGLES

Assemble 24 to 28 bead dangles with the beads and/or pearls of your choice, making the eye pins large enough to fit onto a twisted-wire jump ring. Bead caps are optional.

2 MAKE JUMP RINGS

Create 12 to 14 twisted-wire jump rings, plus 26 to 30 large jump rings and 5 to 7 small jump rings, using 16-gauge wire.

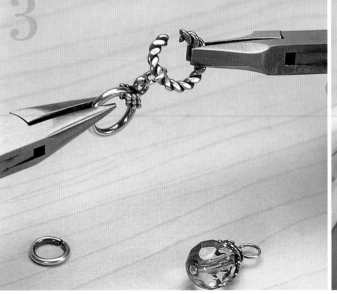

3 ADD JUMP RINGS TO TOGGLE CLASP

To begin the bracelet assembly, place two small jump rings on the round end of the toggle clasp. Open a twisted-wire jump ring and attach it to the end jump ring, as shown.

4 ADD BEAD DANGLES

Place two bead dangles on the twisted-wire jump ring, one on each side of the clasp, followed by two large plain jump rings. Close the twisted-wire jump ring.

5 ADD TWISTED-WIRE JUMP RING AND BEAD DANGLE

Open a second twisted-wire jump ring and run it through the two large plain jump rings. Attach two bead dangles to the twisted-wire jump ring, one on each side of the plain jump rings.

6 ADD TWO PLAIN JUMP RINGS

Place two more large plain jump rings on the twisted-wire jump ring, then close it. Continue with this pattern (steps 5 and 6) until the bracelet is long enough to fit around your wrist comfortably.

7 ATTACH TOGGLE CLASP

When your bracelet reaches the length you desire, open the last twisted-wire jump ring on the end. Connect the bar end of the toggle clasp to the twisted-wire jump ring using three to five small jump rings, as shown.

tips

Because so many beads are used on this bracelet, it can become very heavy. For this reason, use medium-size, light-weight beads or pearls and also consider making the bracelet without bead caps to lighten its weight.

Make more twisted-wire jump rings than are needed for the bracelet. Because they are handmade, they will vary slightly from one another. Choose the jump rings that are the most similar to create your bracelet, and reserve the remainder for another project.

8 ADD COUNTERWEIGHT BEAD

If desired, attach a counterweight bead and/or charm to the end of the bracelet to keep the clasp from riding to the top of your wrist while you wear it. Once it is assembled, you can artificially age your bracelet in a liver-of-sulfur solution.

Jump Ring Choker

Create a jump ring necklace every bit as lovely as your bracelet.

To get started, make jump rings, twisted-wire jump rings, bead or pearl dangles, and bead or pearl connectors using the wire of your choice (gold copper, silver or bronze) and your favorite beads or pearls.

1 JOIN JUMP RINGS

Open one small plain jump ring, run it through the round part of a toggle clasp and one twisted-wire jump ring, then close it. Open the twisted-wire jump ring and slip on two large plain jump rings, then close it. Open another twisted-wire jump ring and run it through the two large plain jump rings. Add two more large plain jump rings and close the twisted-wire jump ring. Continue with this pattern until you have assembled five twisted-wire jump rings, as shown.

2 ADD JUMP RINGS AND BEAD CONNECTORS

Open a twisted-wire jump ring and run it through one end of a bead or pearl connector. Add a bead or pearl dangle, then another bead or pearl connector. Close the jump ring. Continue with this pattern until you have linked together all the bead or pearl connectors. Attach this length to the length made in step 1, connecting the two ends with two plain jump rings.

3 FINISH NECKLACE

On the last bead or pearl connector, add two plain jump rings, then a twisted-wire jump ring. Repeat the pattern to mirror the opposite end, finishing with three small jump rings and the bar end of the toggle clasp.

Linked Hearts Bracelet

This easy project renders elegant results in a single afternoon. The bracelet can be made with just about any type of metal, and you can easily alter the look by using a heavier-gauge wire such as 14 or a lighter gauge such as 18. For a variation on this project, try making a very large heart link with 6″ (15cm) of 14-gauge wire. Use it as the basis for a pendant, or make several links and string them together to fashion a big heart-link choker.

TOOLS AND MATERIALS

jewelry toolkit

16-gauge round wire in your choice of copper, brass, sterling silver or gold

optional:

liver-of-sulfur solution

TECHNIQUES YOU'LL BE USING

Cleaning and Cutting Wire (pages 15–16)

Making a Heart Link (page 44–45)

Making Jump Rings (pages 18–22)

Making a Hook Clasp for Linked Jewelry (page 49)

optional:

Artificially Aging Jewelry (pages 57–58)

Flush cut 14 lengths of 16-gauge wire, each measuring 3" (8cm), for heart links. If you are using different gauges of wire, you may need to adjust the measurements accordingly. Cut additional wire to make coils for 14 large jump rings and 6 small jump rings.

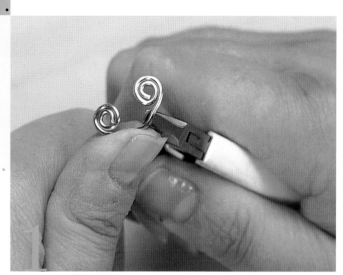

1 MAKE HEART LINKS AND JUMP RINGS

Make 14 heart links, 14 large jump rings and 6 small jump rings. (You may need more or fewer, depending on the size of your wrist.)

2 JOIN HEART-LINK PAIRS

Join two heart links together with one small jump ring, as shown. Make several pairs of joined heart links in this manner, using all the heart links made in step 1.

3 MAKE BRACELET

Hook the heart link pairs together end to end to form a bracelet, as shown. Use large jump rings to connect the top and bottom spirals of each link.

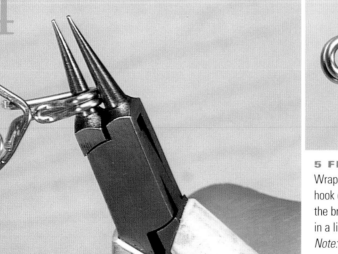

5 FINISH CLASP

Wrap the tails onto the heart link, then around each side of the hook clasp to secure. This will easily hook into the opposite end of the bracelet. Once assembled, you can artificially age your bracelet in a liver-of-sulfur solution.

Note: You cannot artificially age gold wire.

4 MAKE HOOK CLASP

Using 4" (10cm) of 16-gauge wire (in a metal matching the bracelet), make a small hook clasp. Run the tails of the clasp through the pointed end of the last heart link.

Caged Bead Necklace

Big, bold beads counterbalance the weight of the commercial pendant used in this necklace. The design is toned down to simple elegance by the use of repeated caged bead wraps. Try making a matching bracelet using the same bead wraps and beads, but in smaller sizes.

TOOLS AND MATERIALS

jewelry toolkit

16-gauge round wire

pendant and 12 coordinating beads

optional:

liver-of-sulfur solution

TECHNIQUES YOU'LL BE USING

Cleaning and Cutting Wire (pages 15–16)

Making a Caged Bead (page 39)

Making Jump Rings (pages 18–22)

Making a Pendant Suspender (page 54)

Making an *S* Clasp (page 50)

optional:

Artificially Aging Jewelry (pages 57–58)

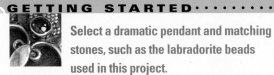

Select a dramatic pendant and matching stones, such as the labradorite beads used in this project.

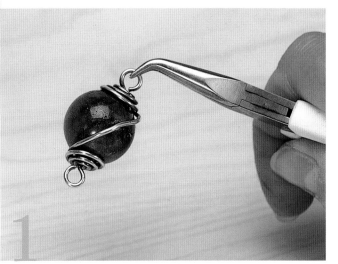

1 WRAP BEADS IN WIRE CAGES

Using 16-gauge wire, make several matching caged beads.

2 CONNECT BEADS

Make several jump rings from 16-gauge wire. Connect the caged beads to one another with doubled jump rings, creating two bead strands that are equal in length. Set the strands aside.

Pendant suspenders are helpful when a commercial pendant isn't easily attached to jump rings. The pendant shown here was designed for a choker-length neck wire, so suspending it was the best option for a necklace linked with jump rings.

3 MAKE PENDANT SUSPENDER

Fashion a pendant suspender on your chosen pendant, as shown (see *Tip*, above). Use doubled jump rings to attach one end of each bead strand to the suspender loops.

4 ADD *S* CLASP

Make an *S* clasp and a couple of easy links. Add an easy link to each end of the necklace, then attach the *S* clasp to one end. Once assembled, you can artificially age your necklace in a liver-of-sulfur solution.

Bead Drop Jewelry

This delicate jewelry set is easy enough to put together in an afternoon. It's so elegant, you'll want to wear it with your dressiest outfits. Keep your beads small, as large and heavy beads will pull on your earlobes and could make your earrings too painful to wear. Even with the most delicate of beads, your Bead Drop Jewelry is sure to turn heads!

TOOLS AND MATERIALS

jewelry toolkit

20-gauge round wire

32 decorative head pins, each 2" (5cm) long

assorted small pearls, beads and crystals

decorative bead caps

necklace chain with clasp

optional:
liver-of-sulfur solution

TECHNIQUES YOU'LL BE USING

Cleaning and Cutting Wire (pages 15–16)

Making Jump Rings (pages 18–22)

Making a Bead Dangle With a Single Eye Pin (page 34)

Making *Shepherd's Hook Earrings* (pages 78–81)

optional:
Artificially Aging Jewelry (pages 57–58)

Using 20-gauge wire, make 32 small jump rings. Select a coordinated assortment of 32 small beads, pearls and crystals to use for the jewelry set.

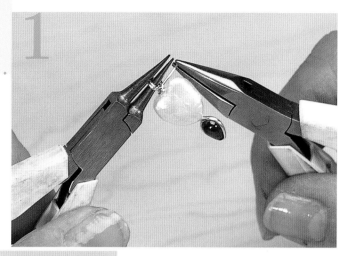

1 ASSEMBLE BEAD DANGLES

Assemble 32 bead dangles in sets of four; 16 will be used to assemble the bead drop pendant and 16 for one pair of bead drop earrings (eight for each earring).

2 BEGIN BEAD DROP PENDANT

Open one jump ring and place one bead dangle on it. Close the jump ring securely. Open a second jump ring and run it through the first jump ring. Place one bead dangle on the second jump ring, then close it.

3 FINISH BEAD DROP PENDANT

Open a third jump ring and place it on the second jump ring, continuing the pattern started in step 2 until you have 16 bead dangles assembled on a chain of 16 small jump rings.

4 ASSEMBLE BEAD DROP EARRINGS

Follow the directions in steps 2 and 3, but instead of making one long dangle, make two, each having eight bead dangles on a chain of eight small jump rings. Fashion ear wires as described in *Shepherd's Hook Earrings* (pages 78–81), then place the bead drop earring dangles on them.

5 PLACE PENDANT ON CHAIN

Place the bead drop pendant on a necklace chain of your choice. Once it is assembled, you can artificially age your jewelry in a liver-of-sulfur solution.

Abstract-Shaped Pin

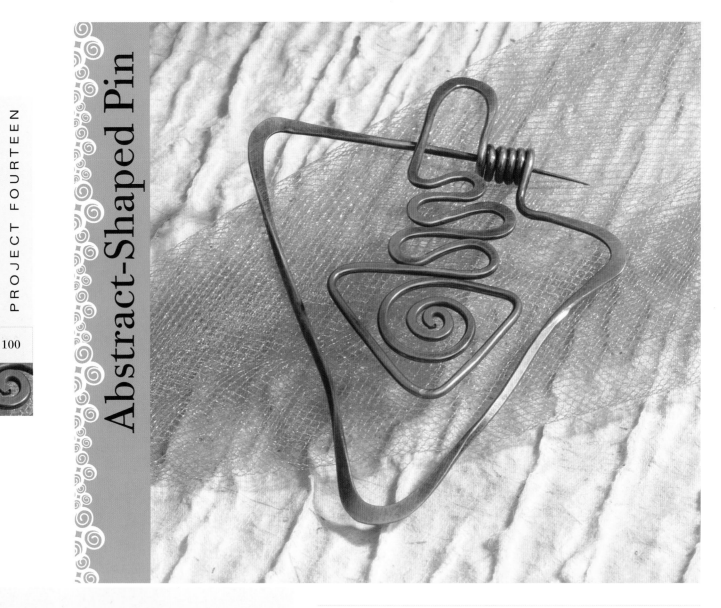

Abstract brooches are, well, abstract! So there's little preparation needed to make these freeform pins. Prime the pump of your imagination, take hold of a piece of wire, then let your fingers take it from there. You'll need little more to create beautiful abstract brooches in a wide array of designs.

TOOLS AND MATERIALS

jewelry toolkit

16- or 14-gauge round wire

optional:

beads and/or charms in various sizes, shapes and colors

liver-of-sulfur solution

TECHNIQUES YOU'LL BE USING

Cleaning and Cutting Wire (pages 15–16)

Making a Spiral (page 17)

Hammering Wire (page 16)

Sharpening and Filing Wire to a Point (page 56)

optional:

Artificially Aging Jewelry (pages 57–58)

Flush cut up to 3' (91cm) of wire.

1 SPIRAL WIRE

Start a spiral in the tips of the small round-nose pliers and continue spiraling the wire about three times using the flat-nose pliers. Do not spiral the wire tightly; instead, leave space between each spiral, as shown.

2 FORM TRIANGLE

When finished spiraling, use the flat-nose pliers to create a sharp 90 degree bend in the wire, followed by another bend to form a triangle around the spiral, as shown.

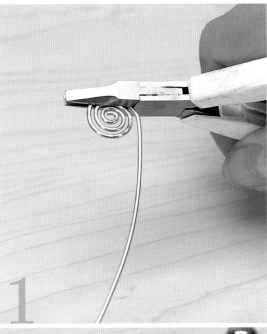

3 SHAPE AND HAMMER WIRE

Shape the wire into a zigzag design above the triangle, and then use a chasing hammer to selectively flatten parts of the wire design. This makes the abstract linear design more interesting and work-hardens the wire.

4 BEND WIRE

Create a sharp 90 degree bend in the wire, then form a long loop over the top of the design. Bring the straight end of the wire all the way over, allowing it to lie on top of the abstract shape, as shown. Flatten the loop with a chasing hammer.

5 COIL WIRE

Grip the straight end of the wire about 1" (25mm) below the top of the loop. Form three to five small coils in the wire at the middle of the small round-nose pliers.

6 SECURE PIN SHAPE

Use the flat-nose pliers to bend the wire down about ½" (13mm) below the coils, then bend the wire again into a desired shape to frame the abstract design. In this piece, I finished with another triangle to echo the interior triangular shape. Hammer the sharp bends in the wire well with the chasing hammer to secure the shape of the pin (see *Tip*, below).

7 CREATE SHARP END

Run the wire end through the coil created in step 5 and then trim the end, making sure that you allow plenty of wire to form a sharp end. Use a chasing hammer and wire cutters to create a sharp pin, then file and polish the pin with 0000 steel wool. Once it is assembled, you can artificially age your pin in a liver-of-sulfur solution.

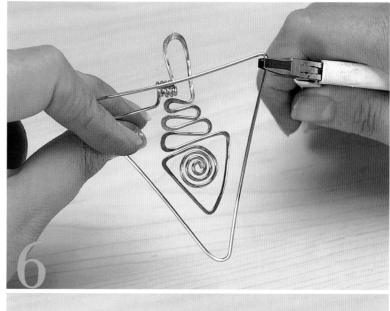

tip

Hammer any part of the pin design that is bent. This will harden it and help the pin keep its shape.

Abstract-Shaped Pins provide the opportunity to really showcase your creativity. Because there is no specific pattern to follow, you are free to be guided by your own creative vision. This is a great project to feature a favorite focal bead or use leftover beads from other projects.

Abstract-Shaped Pin with Beads

If desired, you can accent your abstract design with an interesting selection of beads.

103

When making an Abstract-Shaped Pin, it may help to first sketch out a design before constructing the piece. Be willing, however, to remake your jewelry as you design it. As often as I've tried to sketch out a new design on paper before picking up a piece of wire, I've never been able to make new pieces exactly the way I've pictured them. There's always a bit of trial-and-error. Oftentimes these blunders are blessings, leading me into new, unforeseen directions. I never know what will happen—and that's why I love making jewelry.

Keep a notebook handy as you make your first pins and record the amount of wire used to make each one. This will be of great assistance later when you are attempting to duplicate your pins.

Try making your pin pattern using inexpensive copper wire first. Once you've fashioned a pin that you like, it can be remade using sterling silver or gold wire.

Heart Link Convertible Jewelry

Y You get two for one with this jewelry piece: one long, elegant necklace that converts easily into a short choker and bracelet set. You'll be using heart links in this necklace design, but for added variety try using wrapped eye pin links and/or twisted-wire jump rings, as shown on page 107.

TOOLS AND MATERIALS

jewelry toolkit

16-gauge round wire

decorative head pins

matching beads or pearls

matching decorative beadcaps

optional:

liver-of-sulfur solution

TECHNIQUES YOU'LL BE USING

Cleaning and Cutting Wire (pages 15–16)

Making Jump Rings (pages 18–22)

Making Twisted-Wire Jump Rings (pages 22–23)

Making a Bead Dangle With a Single Eye Pin (page 34)

Making a Bead Connector (pages 36–37)

Making and Joining Easy Links (pages 40–41)

Making a Heart Link (pages 44–45)

Making an *S* Clasp (page 50)

optional:

Artificially Aging Jewelry (pages 57–58)

In addition, for the *Variation:*

Making a Wrapped Eye Pin Link (pages 32–33)

There are lots of links, bead connectors and bead dangles in this convertible necklace set. I recommend organizing the materials for the following components ahead of time: 10 twisted-wire jump rings, 12 large plain jump rings, 5 bead dangles with bead caps, 14 bead connectors, 4 easy links, 11 heart links (5 with bead dangles attached) and 2 *S* clasps.

1 CREATE JUMP RINGS

Create 10 twisted-wire jump rings and 12 large plain jump rings from 16-gauge wire. Make both kinds of jump rings on the back of the extra-long round-nose pliers.

105

2 CREATE BEAD DANGLES AND BEAD CONNECTORS

Assemble five bead dangles using decorative head pins and matching bead caps. Create 14 bead connectors using 16-gauge wire.

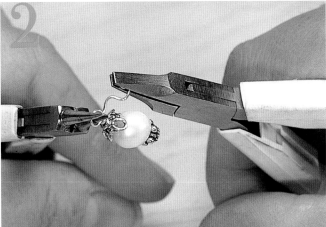

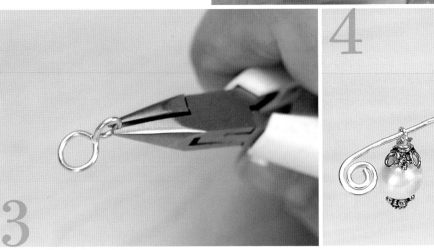

3 CREATE EASY LINKS

Create four easy links from 16-gauge wire.

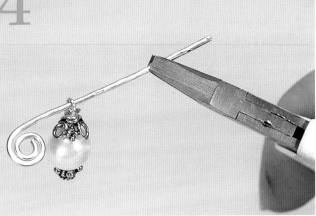

4 MAKE HEART LINKS WITH BEAD DANGLES

Make five heart links from 16-gauge wire and attach a bead dangle to each before finishing the links.

5 BEGIN ASSEMBLING NECKLACE

To assemble the necklace, start at the bottom, linking the five heart links with bead dangles side by side using large, plain jump rings. Attach a twisted-wire jump ring to the heart link on each end with a large, plain jump ring. Before closing the twisted-wire jump rings, add a bead connector to each one.

6 FINISH NECKLACE

Continue the twisted-wire jump ring and pearl connector pattern until the necklace has five twisted-wire jump rings and five bead connectors on each side.

7 ADD *S* CLASP

Add one easy link to each end of the necklace. Make an *S* clasp, then attach it to the easy links, as shown.

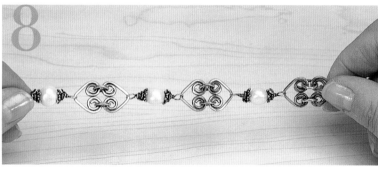

8 ASSEMBLE BRACELET

The back portion of the long necklace (which becomes a bracelet once removed from the necklace) is made by joining bead connectors and heart links. Assemble the bracelet, using the illustration above as a guide. First, make six heart links. Join a pair of heart links by connecting the top spirals and bottom spirals of each link with large, plain jump rings. Next, attach a bead connector to either side of the joined heart links. Continue until you have joined three pairs of heart links with four bead connectors. On each end of the bracelet, attach an easy link. Make an *S* clasp and join it to the easy links on each end of the bracelet, as you did to the necklace in step 7. Once it is assembled, you can artificially age your jewelry set in a liver-of-sulfur solution.

9 CONVERT AS DESIRED

The necklace may be worn long, or it may be converted into a short choker and bracelet set, as shown. To connect the bracelet and the necklace, unclasp each piece of jewelry. Then, attach one end of the necklace with one end of the bracelet, using one *S* clasp. Repeat on the other side, securing the necklace with the second *S* clasp.

Classic Convertible Jewelry

For a completely different look using the same pattern, try making Classic Convertible Jewelry. Instead of using heart links and bead connectors, use twisted-wire jump rings and wrapped eye pin links. This design can also be altered quite dramatically with the use of pearls, crystals or large stone beads.

To get started, make 68 plain jump rings, 23 twisted-wire jump rings, 5 bead dangles, 8 wrapped eye pin links and 2 S clasps.

1 ASSEMBLE BRACELET

Assemble the bracelet by connecting six twisted-wire jump rings to one another with doubled plain jump rings. Add a wrapped eye pin link to each end with doubled plain jump rings, then add a single plain jump ring to each end. Finish with an S clasp.

2 ASSEMBLE NECKLACE

Assemble the necklace, starting at the bottom and using the illustration above as a guide. First, attach five bead dangles to five twisted-wire jump rings, then connect the twisted-wire jump rings to each other with doubled plain jump rings. On each side, attach three sets of wrapped eye pin links connected to twisted-wire jump rings with doubled plain jump rings. Complete the necklace with three more twisted-wire jump rings connected by doubled plain jump rings on each end, followed by a single plain jump ring on each side and an S clasp.

Coiled-Wire Bangle

This bold bangle is based on an ancient coiling technique that goes back to the Egyptians. The project simply repeats the process of making a basic coil until you have a beautiful bracelet. For a variation, use the same amount of wire and add a very large focal bead and a few spacer beads.

TOOLS AND MATERIALS

jewelry toolkit

14-, 18-, 22- and 24-gauge round wire

optional:
liver-of-sulfur solution

TECHNIQUES YOU'LL BE USING

Cleaning and Cutting Wire (pages 15–16)

Hammering Wire (page 16)

Making a Double-Coiled Bead Wrap (pages 30–31)

Making a Simple Eye Pin (pages 24–25)

Making a "Big Hook" Clasp (pages 52–53)

optional:
Artificially Aging Jewelry (pages 57–58)

Flush cut a 280" (711cm) length of 24-gauge wire, a 130" (330cm) length of 22-gauge wire, a 36" (91cm) length of 18-gauge wire, and a 8½" (22cm) length of 14-gauge wire. Hammer the 14-gauge wire with a hard-plastic mallet to work-harden it, then set it aside.

1 MAKE FIRST WRAP

Wrap 280" (711cm) of 24-gauge wire onto a 130" (330cm) mandrel of 22-gauge wire. Bring the long coil to the center of the 22-gauge wire.

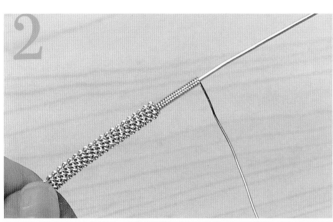

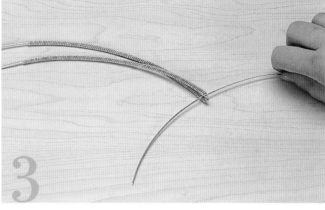

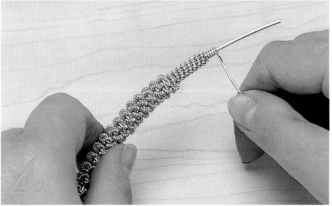

2 MAKE SECOND WRAP

Bend the wire in half, and place it on a 36" (91cm) mandrel of 18-gauge wire. Wrap the coiled wire onto the 18-gauge wire.

3 PLACE DOUBLE-COILED WIRE

Bend the double-coiled wire in half, and place it on an 8½" (22cm) mandrel of 14-gauge wire.

4 MAKE THIRD WRAP

Bring the coiled wire to the center of the 14-gauge wire and wrap it.

5 CREATE BANGLE

On the back of the extra-long round-nose pliers, create an eye pin on each end of the 14-gauge wire. Close both eye pins securely. Create a "big hook" clasp. Open one eye pin and place the clasp on it, then close the eye pin to secure. Once it is assembled, you can artificially age your bracelet in a liver-of-sulfur solution.

Party Watch

It's time to party! These wire-art watches are so much fun to wear, they'll perk up your spirits every time you check the hour.

TOOLS AND MATERIALS

jewelry toolkit

16- and 22-gauge round wire

assorted beads and/or pearls in various sizes and colors

24 decorative head pins

watch head (sterling silver preferred) with loops

toggle clasp

optional:

24 to 48 decorative bead caps

counterweight bead(s) or charm(s)

liver-of-sulfur solution

TECHNIQUES YOU'LL BE USING

Cleaning and Cutting Wire (pages 15–16)

Making Twisted-Wire Jump Rings (pages 22–23)

Hammering Wire (page 16)

Making a Bead Dangle With a Single Eye Pin *or* a Double Eye Pin (pages 34–35)

Making a Bead Connector (pages 36–37)

optional:

Artificially Aging Jewelry (pages 57–58)

Note: If you plan to artificially age your watch, see *Tip* on page 112.

Select coordinating beads for your watch. If possible, choose a watch head with loops large enough to accommodate twisted-wire jump rings.

1 CREATE TWISTED-WIRE JUMP RINGS

Make four twisted-wire jump rings with 16-gauge wire. Hammer them lightly with a chasing hammer, then set them aside.

2 MAKE BEAD DANGLES

Assemble 24 small bead dangles, using the beads or pearls of your choice. Bead caps are optional. Be sure to make large eye pins on each bead dangle so the twisted-wire jump rings can fit through them with ease.

3 MAKE BEAD CONNECTORS

Make at least four bead connectors, using 5" to 6" (13cm to 15cm) of 22-gauge wire. Set them aside.

4 ATTACH TWISTED-WIRE JUMP RINGS TO WATCH HEAD

If the loops on your watch head are large enough, run one twisted-wire jump ring through each loop. Otherwise, run a smaller jump ring made of 22-gauge wire through each watch head loop, then attach bead connectors or twisted-wire jump rings to them.

5 ADD BEAD DANGLES AND CONNECTORS

Before closing the twisted-wire jump rings, add three bead dangles, then one bead connector, then three more bead dangles, to each. Close the twisted-wire jump rings very securely.

6 CONTINUE ADDING TO BRACELET

Add another twisted-wire jump ring to the end of each bead connector, then repeat step 5. Place the watch on your wrist to check the measurement. Add or remove bead connectors or jump rings as needed.

7 ATTACH TOGGLE CLASP

Use jump rings to attach the round end of a toggle clasp to one end of the bracelet. If you enjoy wearing your watch a little loose, attach counterweight beads near the clasp to keep it from riding on top of your wrist.

You must detach the watch head from the bracelet portion of the watch before submerging the bracelet in a liver-of-sulfur solution (as described in the *Techniques* section). Do not submerge the watch head in the solution. Rinse the bracelet portion, allow it to dry and polish it with 0000 steel wool before reattaching it to the watch head. You can tumble-polish this portion of the watch as well, but not the watch head. If you're using a copper or sterling-silver watch head and you would like to artificially age it, dip a cotton swab into the liver-of-sulfur solution and then rub it over the metal watchcase, avoiding the watch face area. Take care not to apply too much solution, which could seep into the watchcase and ruin the watch. Use 0000 steel wool to polish the watchcase with care. The entire watch may be polished with a polishing cloth.

Even if you choose not to artificially age your watch head with the liver-of-sulfur solution, you may want to remove the super-shiny surface on the watchcase by gently rubbing it with 0000 steel wool. I often do this with my watches because I prefer an aged appearance over a sparkly one. Take special care not to rub the steel wool over the glass watch face.

8 FINISH CLASP

Attach the bar end of the toggle clasp to the opposite end of the bracelet. Once it is assembled, you can artificially age your watch in a liver-of-sulfur solution (see *Tip,* above).

Tailor the appearance of your party watch to fit your own individual style. You can give the watch your signature look by using a unique assortment of beads.

Stick-Pearl Watch

Stick pearls are a surprising component in this watch. The pearls' natural color as well as their odd shape and size make for a very interesting timepiece.

Watch heads are available in many styles to suit your taste. The watch-cases may be made of sterling silver, nontarnishing rhodium silver, marcasite, stainless steel, gold or even copper. Look for watch heads with loops instead of pins for connecting the bracelet portion of the watch to the head.

When choosing beads or pearls for this project, consult the color wheel for inspiration. Sometimes a monochromatic (one hue) color scheme is best, as in the Stick-Pearl Watch. Turquoise green looks great with dyed purple pearls. Also, try making a Party Watch with Venetian beads in a rainbow of hues.

Venetian Beads Watch

A watch is the ideal jewelry piece for showing off some of your more expensive beads, such as these Venetian beads from Italy.

S Link Charm Bracelet

Embellished with fanciful charms and bead dangles, this funky bracelet is fun to wear. *S* links with bead dangles make beautiful necklaces as well as bracelets. If you are using *S* links for a necklace (short choker-length recommended), attach bead dangles and/or metal charms to one side of the links only. This allows the necklace to lie nicely on your neck.

TOOLS AND MATERIALS

jewelry toolkit

16-gauge round wire

assorted beads and/or pearls in various sizes and colors

100 decorative head pins

optional:

100 decorative bead caps

counterweight bead(s) or charm(s)

liver-of-sulfur solution

TECHNIQUES YOU'LL BE USING

Cleaning and Cutting Wire (pages 15–16)

Making and Joining *S* Links (pages 41–42)

Making Jump Rings (pages 18–22)

Making a Bead Dangle With a Single Eye Pin *or* a Double Eye Pin (pages 34–35)

Making a Hook Clasp for Linked Jewelry (page 49)

optional:

Artificially Aging Jewelry (pages 57–58)

Select a coordinated mixture of beads and charms for your bracelet. If you are using metal charms, match them to whatever type of metal you are using to create the *S* links.

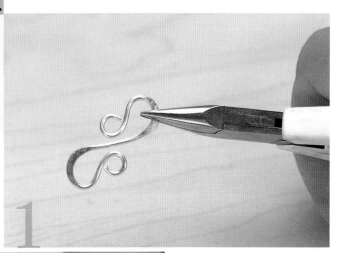

1 MAKE *S* LINKS AND JUMP RINGS

Make several *S* links from 16-gauge wire. (The bracelet pictured on page 114 is made with six *S* links and measures 8" [20cm].) Next, make ten jump rings on the back of the extra-long round-nose pliers.

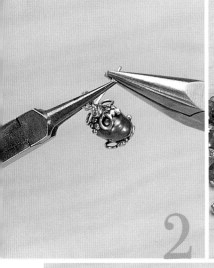

2 CREATE BEAD DANGLES

Create 100 or so bead dangles (bead caps optional) and/or attach several charms to several jump rings.

3 CONNECT *S* LINKS

Connect *S* links to each other with doubled jump rings. Next, add bead dangles and/or charms to the links and jump rings, distributing them throughout the bracelet in a pleasing design.

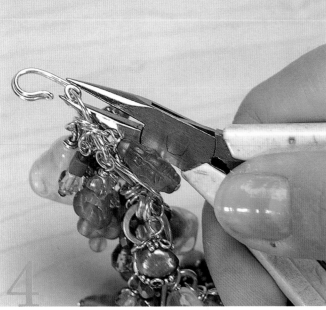

4 ADD CLASP

Using 3" (8cm) of 16-gauge wire, make a small hook clasp. Attach the clasp to the end of the bracelet by running the tails of the clasp through the last jump ring and then wrapping each tail around the jump ring to secure it.

5 ADD COUNTERWEIGHT BEAD

Add a counterweight bead or charm to the clasp area of the bracelet to keep the clasp from riding up to the top of your wrist. Once it is assembled, you can artificially age your bracelet in a liver-of-sulfur solution.

Milagro Charm Necklace

Milagro means "miracle," and these charms are associated with miracles of healing and safety. Usually made of pot metal, they are sold in some bead stores, at bead shows and in many South American towns. Better stores will offer the charms in sterling silver.

TOOLS AND MATERIALS

jewelry toolkit

wire (your choice), sufficient for making caged beads and coiled bead wraps

wire (your choice), sufficient for making wrapped eye pin links, jump rings and additional wire links

beads in various sizes, shapes and colors

sterling silver Milagro charms

pendant

optional:

   decorative bead caps

   liver-of-sulfur solution

TECHNIQUES YOU'LL BE USING

Cleaning and Cutting Wire (pages 15–16)

Making Jump Rings (pages 18–22)

Making a Pendant Suspender (page 54)

optional:

   Artificially Aging Jewelry (pages 57–58)

Suggested techniques for necklace components:

Making a Bead Dangle With a Single Eye Pin (page 34)

Making a Caged Bead (page 39)

Making a Bead Connector (pages 36–37)

Making a Single-Coiled Bead Wrap (pages 28–30)

Making a Double-Coiled Bead Wrap (pages 30–31)

Making a Coiled-Wire Bead Wrap (pages 37–38)

Making a Double-Coiled Wire Bead Wrap (page 38)

Making a Wrapped Eye Pin Link (pages 32–33)

A lot of planning goes into a necklace design of this complexity. Consider the beads, charms and pendant you'd like to use, then plan out your design meticulously before you begin construction.

1 SELECT BEADS AND MAKE NECKLACE COMPONENTS

Select beads and plan your necklace design. Make bead dangles, caged beads, coiled-wire bead wraps, bead connectors, wrapped eye pin links and any other accent pieces you may want to incorporate into the necklace.

2 BEGIN WITH PENDANT

Start with the pendant. Create and attach a pendant suspender if necessary. On either side of the pendant, attach a small caged bead. Add jump rings to the eye pins of the caged bead, then add more beads, bead dangles and accent pieces in the desired order.

3 CONTINUE TO ADD EMBELLISHMENTS

Continue adding wrapped beads, wrapped eye pins, jump rings and additional links as desired until you have created a 28" (71cm)-long necklace.

117

4 ADD MILAGRO CHARMS

Using jump rings, add Milagro charms to the outside of the necklace where it seems most appropriate. This necklace does not require a clasp because it is so long.

5 FINISH WITH BRIDGES

If desired, add "bridges" of wire links and bead wraps with dangling Milagro charms to the necklace, as shown. Once it is assembled, you can artificially age your necklace in a liver-of-sulfur solution.

Twin-Spiral Bracelet

This is a heavy-duty bracelet! Made of 14-gauge round wire in sterling silver, it's substantial and durable. Because 14-gauge wire is somewhat heavy, I often switch to 16-gauge wire when I'm making twin-spiral necklaces. You also can try substituting less-expensive brass or copper wire for the silver.

TOOLS AND MATERIALS

jewelry toolkit

14-, 16-, 20- and 22-gauge round wire

optional:

liver-of-sulfur solution

TECHNIQUES YOU'LL BE USING

Cleaning and Cutting Wire (page 15–16)

Making a Spiral (page 17)

Hammering Wire (page 16)

Making a Hook Clasp for Linked Jewelry (page 49)

optional:

Artificially Aging Jewelry (pages 57–58)

When you are making this jewelry piece, accurate measurements are critically important. Before beginning the project, you may want to review all the steps first, then measure and flush cut the wire lengths you'll be needing.

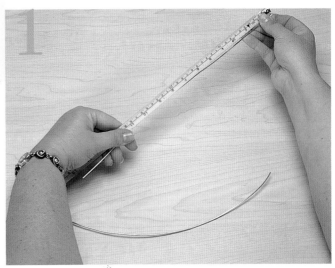

1 CUT WIRE
Measure and flush cut two 15" (38cm) lengths of 14-gauge wire.

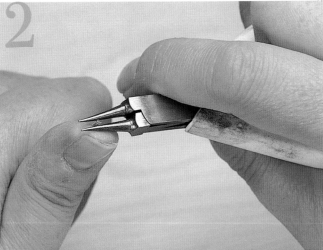

2 GRIP WIRE
Grip one end of a 15" (38cm) wire length in the middle of your small round-nose pliers. This is the beginning of a spiral with a large center hole.

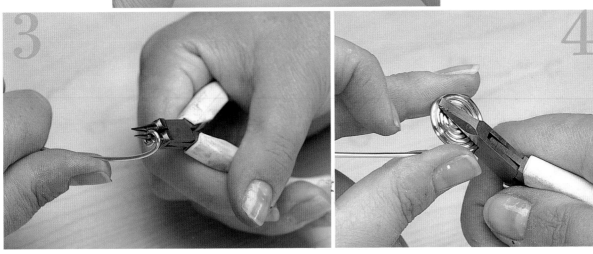

3 START SPIRAL
Roll your wrist forward, bending the wire until it forms a *U* shape around the jaw of the pliers. Open the tool, rotate your hand backward and close down on the wire. With a quick twist of the wrist, rotate your hand forward to create the beginning of a spiral.

4 CONTINUE SPIRAL
Grip the spiral between the flat-nose pliers, then continue spiraling the wire in tiny increments.

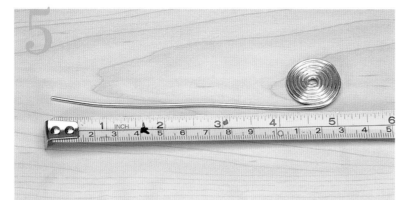

5 FINISH SPIRALING ONE END
Spiral the wire until the piece measures exactly 5" (13cm) from end to end.

6 SPIRAL OTHER END
Use the same technique to spiral the opposite end of the wire inward. Continue until the two spirals meet.

7 HAMMER SPIRALS
Hammer the wire with a hard-plastic mallet on a steel bench block, then hammer the wire *lightly* with a chasing hammer. Do not overdo the hammering, as you do not want to flatten the spirals.

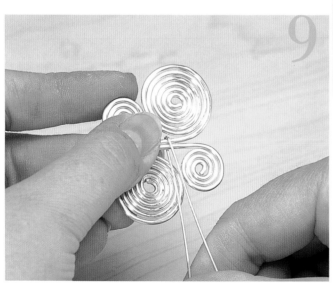

8 POSITION SPIRAL WIRE LENGTHS
Make an identical double-spiral length with the remaining wire. When finished, place the double spirals on your work surface, with the straight lengths facing each other, the large spiral ends diagonal to each other and the small spiral ends diagonal to each other, as shown.

9 BEND WIRE OVER CENTER
Flush cut a 7" (18cm) length of 22-gauge wire. Bend the wire over the two spiral wire lengths at the center, as shown.

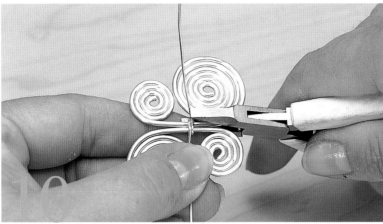

10 WRAP TAILS AROUND CENTER

Wrap each tail of the wire around the center of the two spiral wire lengths, using the flat-nose pliers to bend the wire and press it into position.

11 CONTINUE WRAPPING WIRE AROUND CENTER

Continue wrapping the wire. Take your time to make sure that as the wire is wrapped, the coils are placed flush, side by side. While wrapping, hold the spirals in position to keep the two pieces together.

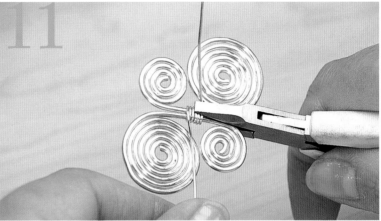

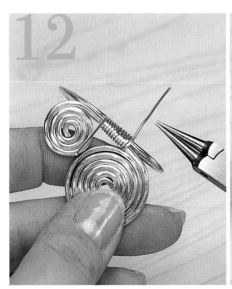

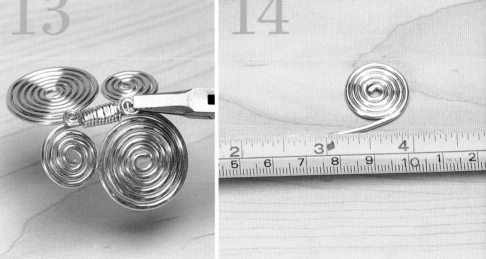

12 FINISH WRAPPING AND TRIM

Wrap the wire around the center 12 times. When finished, measure the wire tails that remain. If necessary, trim the tails so that they are equal in length.

13 ADD SPIRALS

Spiral each tail, then use the flat-nose pliers to press the spiraled tails flat against the wire unit, as shown. You now have one twin-spiral unit.

14 CREATE MORE SPIRAL LENGTHS

Flush cut four lengths of 14-gauge wire, each measuring 10" (25cm). Repeat steps 1 to 7, this time using a 10" (25cm) length of wire. In the fifth step, spiral the wire until the piece measures exactly 4" (10cm) from end to end.

15 POSITION TWO UNITS

Repeat steps 8 to 13, this time binding the two spiral lengths together with a 5" (13cm) length of 22-gauge wire. When finished, lay this unit on your work surface, with the larger unit placed immediately to the left. The two units should mirror each other, as shown.

16 CUT AND MARK WIRE FOR CONNECTOR

Flush cut two 4" (10cm) lengths of 14-gauge wire for the connector. Use a permanent marker to mark both lengths 1½" (4cm) from each end, leaving 1" (25mm) in the center of each length.

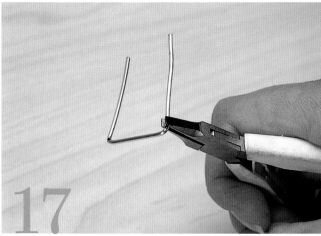

17 BEND CONNECTOR UP

Using the marks as a guide, bend up the left and right ends of each wire length, as shown.

18 JOIN UNITS WITH CONNECTOR

Join the two units with the connector wire, placing the left end through the center opening of the spiral on the left side and the right end through the center opening of the spiral on the right side, as shown. Once the connector is in position, there should be a slight gap between the two units.

19 BEND CONNECTOR DOWN

Bend down each end of the connector wire, pressing them flat against the spiral surface with the flat-nose pliers.

20 SPIRAL ENDS

Cross one end of the connector over the other and twist to form a link, then spiral in each end to form a figure 8, as shown. Create another unit with small spirals, then join it to the unit with the large spirals in the same manner. You should have three joined units in all.

21 BEGIN THE CLASP

Flush cut a 6" (15cm) length of 16-gauge wire. Use this wire to create a hook clasp.

22 ATTACH CLASP TO ONE END

Run the tails of the clasp through the center of the last spiral on one end of the bracelet, as shown.

23 SEPARATE TAILS

Separate the tails into a V shape on the other side of the spiral.

24 FOLD TAILS OVER

Using flat-nose pliers, fold each tail over to the opposite side of the spiral, positioning one tail on either side of the clasp hook. Press both tails against the surface of the spiral.

Because you are manipulating the wire so much in this project, you'll find that the wire will become extremely work-hardened. This will make the wire increasingly difficult to bend and shape as you progress through the project. Prepare yourself for this and any other jewelry-making challenges by always using good-quality tools.

25 FINISH ENDS

Make a decorative loop at the end of each tail and press each loop against the surface of the spiral.

26 WRAP CLASP HOOK

Flush cut a 4½" to 5" (11 to 13cm) length of 20-gauge wire. Wrap the wire around the straight body of the clasp hook. With each wrap, press the coil onto the wire with the flat-nose pliers. When finished wrapping, trim any remaining wire from the top. Spiral the end and press it flush against the body of the clasp, as shown.

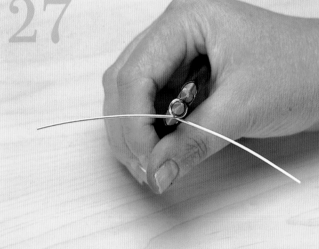

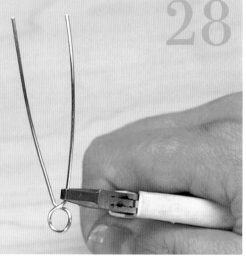

27 CUT WIRE AND FORM LOOP

Flush cut a 6" (15cm) length of 16-gauge wire. Measure the center point of the wire, then grip it with the round-nose pliers. Wrap each end of the wire around the jaw of the pliers to form a single loop.

28 BEND TAILS DOWN

At the base of the loop, bend down each tail with the flat-nose pliers, as shown.

29 BEND TAILS

Measure ⅝" (16mm) from the base of the loop, then bend both tails at a 90 degree angle, as shown.

30 RUN TAILS THROUGH BASE OF LOOP

Run the bent tails of the loop through the center of the last spiral on the other end of the bracelet. Bend the tails up and press them against the surface of the spiral. Then, run each tail through the opening under the base of the loop, as shown.

31 SPIRAL ENDS

Spiral in the ends of the tails for a decorative finish, then press each against the surface of the large spiral with the flat-nose pliers, as shown.

32 FLATTEN LOOP

Flatten the loop with a chasing hammer on a steel bench block. Once it is assembled, you can artificially age your bracelet in a liver-of-sulfur solution.

Resources

Please support your local bead shops by purchasing all your tools, wire, beads and related supplies from them. By keeping their doors open, you'll be doing yourself a favor. That's because bead stores are the best source of quality instruction from local and visiting instructors. Their knowledgeable staff can assist you with bead selection and jewelry construction, answering your questions and helping you in ways that an online supplier cannot. Nevertheless, it's true that not every store will have everything you need to make every jewelry piece you have in mind. For this reason, I have provided the manufacturer's information of the products that were used in this publication so you can find out where they distribute their wares near you. The Web sites contain technical product support and useful information as well.

Supplies

Africa Direct
(303) 316-7570
www.africadirect.com
beads, beadwork and jewelry dating from antiquity

Ands Silver
(972) 761-0440
www.andssilver.com
silver beads and findings

Eurotool, Inc.
(800) 552-3131
www.eurotool.com
jewelry tools

Fire Mountain Gems and Beads
(800) 355-2137
www.firemountaingems.com
beads, findings, wire

JK Findings
(866) 346-3464
www.jkfindings.com
beads, sterling silver jewelry findings

Natural Touch Beads
(707) 781-0808
www.naturaltouchbeads.com
resin beads

Ott-Lite TrueColor Lighting
(800) 842-8848
www.ottlite.com
natural lighting systems for artists and crafters

Pacific Silverworks
(805) 641-1394
www.pacificsilverworks.com
beads, findings, sterling silver clasps

Pema Arts
(510) 965-9956
www.tibetanbeads.com
Tibetan beads

Priya Imports, Inc.
(800) 869-9240
www.priyaimportsinc.com
beads, Bali and Indian sterling silver beads and findings

Rio Grande
(800) 545-6566
www.riogrande.com
Lindstrom pliers and flush cutters, wide assortment of jewelry tools, beads, findings, display products, liver of sulfur, polishing cloths

Riverstone Bead Company
(219) 939-2050
www.riverstonebead.com
drilled river stones for jewelry making

Shipwreck Beads
(800) 950-4232
www.shipwreck-beads.com
beads, findings, sterling silver, books

Somerset Silver
(425) 641-3666
www.somerset-silver.com
direct importers of hill-tribe silver beads and findings

Sweet Creek Creations
(541) 997-0109
www.sweetcreek.com
Peruvial opal (pink and blue) beads, Bali silver, gold beads, copper beads, silver pendants

Thunderbird Supply
(800) 545-7968
www.thunderbirdsupply.com
wire (sterling silver, copper, brass, gold), beads, findings, tools, liver of sulfur

Tribal Eye
www.oldbeads.com
beads and jewelry dating from antiquity to modern times, specializing in tribal beads

Urban Maille Chain Works
(303) 838-7432
www.urbanmaille.com
Sterling silver jump rings, kits, chainmaille jewelry instruction

Publications

Art Jewelry Magazine
(800) 446-5489
www.artjewelrymag.com
articles on jewelry making, including wire-art jewelry

Bead & Button
(800) 446-5489
www.beadandbutton.com
articles on beading and jewelry making, including wire-art jewelry

Belle Armoire, Art to Wear
(877) 782-6737
www.bellearmoire.com
articles on wearable art, including handmade clothing, beading and wire-art jewelry

Index

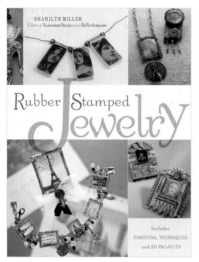

Rubber Stamped Jewelry

ISBN-13: 978-1-58180-384-6, paperback, 128 pages, #32415
ISBN-10: 1-58180-384-2, paperback, 128 pages, #32415

This book combines the self-expressive qualities of rubber stamping with the elegance of jewelry making. Through easy-to-follow instructions and beautiful full-color photos, Sharilyn Miller provides all the invaluable tips and techniques you need to create earrings, necklaces, bracelets and brooches using a wide array of materials like fabric, shrink plastic and more. The book also includes 20 projects from the author and contributing artists.

128

Art to Wear

ISBN-13: 978-1-58180-597-0, paperback, 96 pages, #33110
ISBN-10: 1-58180-597-7, paperback, 96 pages, #33110

There's no better way to show off your creative talents than to adorn yourself, your family and friends with your own works of art. Whatever your unique style, this book shows you how to create jewelry, accessories and clothing that match your personality. Author Jana Ewy demonstrates how to dress up jackets, sweaters, t-shirts, flip-flops, purses and belts with paint, ink, metal, fabric, fibers, beads and even Chinese coins.

Home & Garden Metalcrafts

ISBN-13: 978-1-58180-330-3, paperback, 96 pages, #32296
ISBN-10: 1-58180-330-3, paperback, 96 pages, #32296

With 15 fun and functional metalcraft projects for the home and garden, this book is a must-buy for anyone looking to explore metal's creative decorating possibilities. Inside you'll find step-by-step directions for popular and innovative metal crafting techniques—from texturing, embossing and antiquing metal, to coiling wire and embellishing with beads. Make the most of metal's magical look with great projects, including garden stakes, placemats, a desk set and more.

These and other fine North Light books are available at your local art & craft retailer, bookstore or online supplier.

Simply Beautiful Beading

ISBN-13: 978-1-58180-563-5, paperback, 128 pages, #33018
ISBN-10: 1-58180-563-2, paperback, 128 pages, #33018

Beads give a sense of glamour and fun to everything—jewelry, fabrics and home décor. Author Heidi Boyd will inspire you with over 50 affordable and fashionable projects, including necklaces and bracelets, picture frames, journals and more. Beginners will learn basic beading and jewelry-making techniques, all of which are quick and easy. This book is part of the Simply Beautiful series, which features a simple yet sophisticated approach to popular crafts.